King Salmon:
A Guide To Salmon Fishing in California

Greg Goddard

Printed in the United States of America
First Edition
Charts and maps by Allan Cartography, Medford, Oregon
Book design and typography by One Vogt Graphics, Eureka, California
Cover design by One Vogt Graphics, Eureka, California
Illustrations by Hippo Lau, and Bob Halal
Queen Salmon excerpts used with permission – by David Simpson and Jane Lapiner
Copy editing by Barbara Armentrout

ISBN 0-939837-38-2

Published by
Paradise Cay Publications
P.O. Box 29
Arcata, California, 95521
800-736-4509
707-822-9163 fax
www.paracay.com

King Salmon:
A Guide To Salmon Fishing in California

Greg Goddard

Other Books from Paradise Cay Publications...

COST CONSCIOUS CRUISER 29.95

by Lin and Larry Pardey,
In this book Lin & Larry discuss topics ranging from making your getaway plans to finding a truly affordable boat, keeping your outfitting costs and maintenance time in control, then learning to feel confident as you cruise farther ahead.

THE CAPABLE CRUISER 32.00

by Lin & Larry Pardey
The Capable Cruiser illustrates how successful cruising is the result of a combination of factors including a homogeneous crew, proper preparation, solid gear, regular maintenance and exemplary seamanship.

CARE AND FEEDING OF SAILING CREW 35.00

by Lin & Larry Pardey
This book tells not only how to buy, provision and stow food for local cruising and extended voyages, but also how to take care of all the other aspects of crew comfort.

CRUISING IN SERAFFYN 16.95

by Lin & Larry Pardey

DETAILS OF CLASSIC BOAT CONSTRUCTION: THE HULL 39.95

by Larry Pardey
Building a wooden hull is discussed in detail.

SERAFFYN'S EUROPEAN ADVENTURE 16.95

by Lin & Larry Pardey
Join Lin and Larry while they winter in England working to pay for the next leg of their journey into the Baltic, Denmark, Sweden, Finland, Germany.

SERAFFYN'S MEDITERRANEAN ADVENTURE 16.95

by Lin & Larry Pardey
Seraffyn's Mediterranean Adventure covers three years of cruising life, in and around the Mediterranean.

THE CHINESE SAILING RIG: DESIGN-ING & BUILDING YOUR OWN 15.95

by Derek Van Loan with Dan Haggerty
A practical handbook which emphasizes adapting western hulls to a Chinese rig.

CRUISING CHEF COOKBOOK 2ND EDITION 19.95

by Michael Greenwald
Hundreds of tips plus more than 300 delicious recipes.

A CRUISING GUIDE FROM ACAPULCO TO THE PANAMA CANAL 29.95

by Charles & Nancy Goodman
Detailed descriptions of 51 Anchorages between Acapulco and the Panama Canal.

CRUISING GUIDE TO THE HAWAIIAN ISLANDS 29.95

by Bob and Carolyn Mehaffy
The most comprehensive guide to the Hawaiian Islands ever published.

CRUISING GUIDE TO SAN FRANCISCO BAY, 2ND EDITION 24.95

by Bob & Carolyn Mehaffy
This comprehensive cruising guide includes four more destinations outside the Bay: Pillar Point Harbor, Drakes Bay, Bodega Harbor, and Tomales Bay.

BREATHTAKING – ONE MAN, ONE WOMAN, ONE BOAT: TWO HAPPY DAYS 12.95

by J.P. Valdury
A good humored romp.

ON THE BOULEVARD OF GALLEONS 14.95

by Wallace B. Farrell & Sandra J. Burns
The account of a two-year sailing adventure retracing the paths of Spanish treasure ships and buccaneers in the New World.

SPRING TIDES 14.95

by Ed Larson
Spring Tides speaks of the adventure and beauty of Alaska.

SURVIVOR 26.95

by Michael Greenwald
A boat disaster anthology so gripping you won't be able to put it down. True stories.

TAKING TERRAPIN HOME: A LOVE AFFAIR WITH A SMALL CATAMARAN 14.95

by Mathew Wilson
An exciting account of crossing the Atlantic in a small sailboat.

100 PROBLEMS IN CELESTIAL NAVIGATION 14.95

by Leonard Cray
A potpourri of celestial navigation exercises, each designed around a specific journey.

THE COMPASS BOOK 12.95

by Mike Harris
An introduction to the principles of compass work.

NAUTICAL ALMANAC 17.95

Edited by Matt Morehouse
The cornerstone for all sight reduction.

NAVIGATION RULES (RULES OF THE ROAD) 8.95

Required on board all vessels 12 meters or more in length.

THE STAR FINDER BOOK 12.95

by David Burch
Explains the use of the 2102D star finder, and the many applications it offers.

DRUG TESTING 12.95

by Captain Alan Spears Esq.

HOW TO SURVIVE WITH A POWER-SURVIVOR WATERMAKER

by Gary E. Albers aboard S/V ISHI
How to choose, install, maintain and rebuild the popular PÚR PowerSurvivor watermakers.

LANDFALL LEGALESE - VOLUME I: THE PACIFIC 29.95

Captain Alan Spears, Esq.

VOLUME II: THE CARIBBEAN 24.95

Captain Alan Spears, Esq.
A compendium of the legal requirements and protocols for entering and clearing the majority of popular cruising ports throughout the Pacific and the Caribbean.

SHIPPING OUT 12.95

by Captain Alan Spears, Esq.
An exposé of commercial and recreational shipboard jobs.

DRAG DEVICE DATA BASE 36.95

by Victor Shane
Effective use at sea of parachutes, sea anchors and drogues.

STORM TACTICS HANDBOOK: MODERN METHODS OF HEAVING-TO FOR SURVIVAL IN EXTREME CONDITIONS 19.95

by Lin & Larry Pardey
Modern methods of heaving-to for survival in extreme conditions. Trysail and para-anchor technology for all types of boats and sailors.

Acknowledgments

I could not have written this book by myself. I needed some help and received it from many people. My wife, Miguelina, has supported me through many years of fishing, research, and writing this book, including typing much of the manuscript. My grandfather Louis "Cooc" Matlin taught me the love of fishing at an early age, and both my mom, Seema, and my dad, Howard (better known as "Gat"), supported my fishing throughout my childhood. My father and I shared a strong bond and common experience around salmon fishing, especially during his last years.

My daughter Vari caught her first salmon at age 11 on my sailboat and has shared many trips on the ocean, where she always seems to be the lucky one who lands a nice salmon. My daughter Heather has been very supportive of my fishing, especially with respect to eating the fresh salmon, and she always out-fishes her boyfriends. Heather also helped me with typing the manuscript. My youngest daughter, Camila, has been fishing with me since the age of 4 and loves the sea, especially the sea lions, porpoises, jellyfish, and pelicans.

My long education in salmon fishing started back in the early 1960's, when I hung out on the docks with the skiff fishermen at Pedro Point. After becoming skilled at catching salmon there, I advanced to buying a commercial boat and learning from the professionals at Fisherman's Wharf in San Francisco and in Bodega Bay. My partner at that time, Ed Vickery, passed on to me his key knowledge garnered from working as a deckhand on a commercial salmon troller.

I have had the opportunity to fish and learn with many excellent fisherman, among them are Andy Martin on the *Lots of Lox* and Andy Petterson on the *Louellen*. My boat is berthed at Gas House Cove in San Francisco, where many excellent fisherman have shared their knowledge and experience with me. Special thanks to Eddie Tavasieff, Rich Shears, Ski Ratto, Fred Brunswig, Doug Kyono, and Abe and Angelo Cuanang.

My fishing partners also deserve mention for the shared experiences that have become part of my knowledge. Special thanks to Frank Casey, Michael Missakian, Bart Ribotta, Tom O'Hara, Jon French, Michael Berg, Donald Forrest, and Michael Golden.

I would like to thank Barbara Armentrout who used her professional editing skills to help me with writing and organizing the manuscript. My cousin Stuart Allan helped with advice on maps and charts. Hippo Lau and Bob Halal did the beautiful, artistic diagrams. Thanks to Lon Tokunaga for his Website photos of rigging anchovies. Mike Watson of Barfonline, the Bay Area Regional Fishermen's Web page at <http://www.barfonline.com>, networked key people for me and read the manuscript. Thanks to Bryan Dalton for his story of the 52-pounder that did not get away. Alfred Kuo helped me develop details about techniques and helped edit parts of the manuscript. Perry Kerson of G and M Sales gave advice and read the manuscript. Thanks also to Bat Batsford for reading the manuscript and to Joe Hanson for reading it from the perspective of a Michigan fisherman. I would also like to thank Brian Hoffman, who does the *San Francisco Chronicle* Fishing Report, and Craig Hanson, who writes the "Private Boaters' Spotlight" for *Western Outdoor News,* for reading the manuscript.

Finally, I want to thank Matt Morehouse for publishing this book and making it available to those who love nature, the ocean, and salmon.

This book was written over many years, and salmon regulations have changed and are continuing to change. Please consult the latest DFG regulations and do whatever you can to help preserve our natural resources.

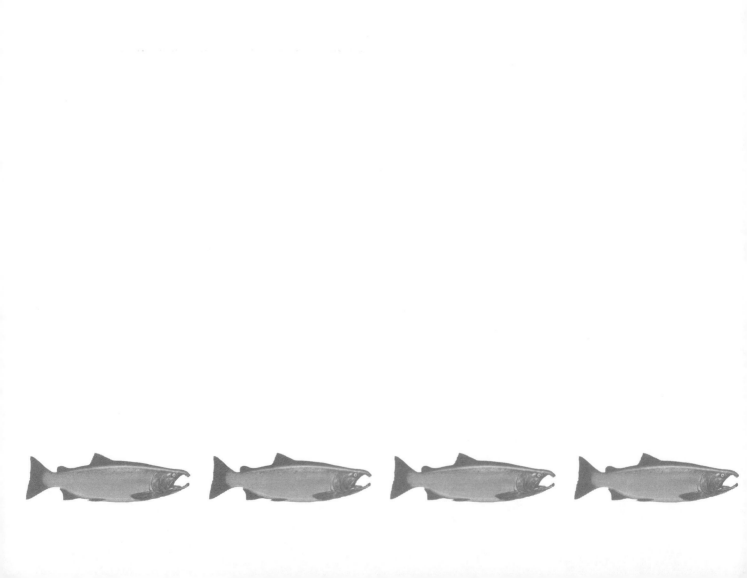

Table of Contents

Chapter 1: Going Salmon Fishing

"Fishing is hunting."
– Jacques Cousteau

It's July and the salmon have made their annual appearance off the coast of San Francisco. From Marin County down to San Mateo County, along the inshore reefs from just outside the breakers to a couple of miles out, the salmon have made their move to feed on the spawning anchovies.

Reports have been coming in all week that big 15- to 30-pound king salmon are being caught up and down the coast. I can feel the excitement build as I contemplate what I need to do to get ready for tomorrow morning's trip.

I've already checked my tackle, put fresh line on my reels, and gone through my tackle box to make sure I'll have the right hooks, leaders, lures, sinkers, releases—everything I'll need for my trip tomorrow. I've called several people to get reports on how they've done, exactly where they fished, how deep, what they were using, and how big the fish were.

I turn on my weather radio to get the weather report. Tomorrow will be "low fog, winds to 15 knots, and flat seas," ideal conditions for salmon fishing.

As I go to bed in anticipation of getting up at 5 a.m., I can hardly sleep thinking about catching a big salmon. The minute the alarm goes off, I jump out of bed and throw on the clothes I got out the night before, including my "lucky shirt" for catching salmon. All fishermen are superstitious; they all have "lucky" somethings, whether it be a shirt, hat, or lure.

The Golden Gate Bridge as seen from the water near Point Bonita looking back to San Francisco.

I go downstairs, open the front door, and look outside to check the weather. There's hardly any breeze, it's foggy—conditions look great. I turn on the weather radio again while I put a pot of water on the stove for coffee, and the report is the same as the night before: "Good conditions. Fog and calm seas."

I throw my gear into the back of my pickup and head for the San Francisco Marina, about a 10-minute trip early in the morning. There's no traffic as I hop on the freeway and travel through the fog-shrouded city.

As I approach the marina, the fog carries the smell of saltwater. I stop in front of the gate where I keep my boat, jump out of the truck, and load my equipment on the dock. The dock is wet. Everything is dripping wet with fog: the boat, the windshields, the gates. A lone night heron takes off from the dock with a screech as I approach. Gulls hover overhead screaming. There's an air of excitement as several other anglers begin to load their boats, getting ready for the morning trek out to the salmon grounds. Boat engines start up and fill the air with the smell of diesel and gas exhaust. Everyone is full of optimism at the prospect of great fishing.

I go through the checklist to make sure the boat is ready for the trip. First I check the bilge to make sure there is no water. Then I check the fuel, the oil, the fish finder, the VHF radio, and the GPS navigation instrument to make sure they're all working. I start the engine and let it warm up while my friend Jon and I unfasten the lines and get the boat ready to make way.

The water is calm as glass as we slowly edge out of the harbor, making sure we do not cause a wake to rock the boats that are still tied up. Low fog hangs over the buildings and keeps the air calm. As we head out the entrance of the harbor, the water changes. There's a big outgoing tide and a little breeze on the water. The strong tide bends the buoy outside the harbor like it's being pulled out toward the Golden Gate Bridge. We slowly pick up speed as we head toward the bridge. We can see only the bottom third; the top is hidden in fog. Underneath the fog, we can see all the way to Point Bonita on the Marin Coast.

We head for the south tower of the bridge. The water becomes rough as the outgoing tide hits the reef in front of the tower. The waves get short and steep, and we have to slow down to go through them. We enter an area of "popcorn" water, which is white from being popped up out of the ocean by the force of tides meeting each other. The tides also create large whirlpools that can turn a small boat around. We slowly cross this area, and the water smooths out as we head for our next landmark, Point Bonita, barely visible about a mile ahead underneath the fog.

Seamen from all over the world know Point Bonita. Here, where the water from the bay meets the rough seas of the Pacific Ocean, huge waves can develop and conditions can be very rough.

At Point Bonita the seas begin to build, and we have to slow down to get around the rough waters caused by the tidal action. After several minutes, conditions start to calm down as we head north toward Duxbury Buoy, which marks a reef off the Marin County coast. (Our compass heading is about 270 degrees, which is actually west.) This area is traditionally a prime holding spot for bait fish and salmon this time of year.

As we get farther from Point Bonita, the water calms down and becomes flat as a lake. We start looking for signs of salmon as we pass Muir Beach on the inside and the "potato patch," a dangerous sandbar also known as Four Fathom Shoals, on the outside.

Gulls, cormorants, and murres on top of a large school of anchovies.

We see a few flocks of scattered murres, black and white duck-like birds. In the distance a pelican dives into the water with a splash , and several gulls follow it down and try to pick up wounded anchovies that it didn't get.

As we approach Duxbury Buoy, we see lines of debris in the water caused by the tidal rips. More and more murres appear. Some carry wiggling anchovies in their beaks as they dive into schools of anchovies below the surface. Several porpoises appear by the bow of our boat and cross in front of us. Several pelicans dive into the water, scooping up mouthfuls of anchovies. Our excitement rises as we see many boats, some with fish bending their rods and several with their nets held at ready. We decide to stop just in front of a large flock of murres that seems to be feeding over a school of anchovies.

Murres have a symbiotic relationship with salmon. They both work schools of anchovies—the murres from the top and the salmon from below. Usually, the smaller salmon attack the school of anchovies and drive it toward the surface. The murres, which can see great distances underwater and can dive down to 80 feet, feed on the anchovies from the top. The large salmon, the lazy ones, lay in wait beneath the school of anchovies for the wounded or dead ones to come floating down to them, where they lazily feed, not expending any energy and getting fatter and fatter.

Today, we will be drift fishing, or "mooching," that is, using light tackle with a dead anchovy placed on the hook with a 1-ounce sinker on a sliding plastic sleeve. Because the bait seems near the surface, we start fishing at 20 feet. But we put down some lines to 25 feet and others to 30 feet to cover different depths where the fish might be.

As my line gets down to 20 feet, I put the reel in gear. Immediately, I feel the tug, tug, tug of a salmon starting to feed on the anchovy. I put the reel in free-spool and again feel the resistance of weight. I put the reel in gear, take up the slack, and as soon as I feel the stiff resistance of the fish, I lift the rod tip and feel the pull of a large salmon shaking its head. As the salmon becomes aware of the hook and the force of the rod, it makes a 50-yard run toward the horizon—line peeling off the reel. The salmon stops, turns its head, and I can sense the power of its big body as it shakes and plays itself against the current, pulling more line off the reel.

After five minutes I gain on the salmon, and it approaches the boat. The net is ready and I slowly bring the tiring salmon toward the boat. As soon as it sees the boat, it puts its head down and makes another long run—peeling 50 or 60 feet of line off the reel. This scenario is repeated two or three times: As the salmon approaches the boat, it sees the net and makes a run. But the runs are getting shorter as the salmon tires and starts to lay on its side. As it circles in toward the boat, the net is made ready and then is scooped under the fish. We have an 18-pound salmon on board, flopping. After a quick blow to the head to subdue it, we carefully put our catch into the fish box. The first salmon is in the boat.

It is a beautiful fish. It glistens with iridescence as it comes out of the water, a bronze-silver color with purply hues. Sea lice are attached to the underside, just behind the anal fin. We can tell that this 18-pound fish is a male, because its lower jaw has a slight hook and it is a little longer and skinnier than the female.

An example of a 12-pound salmon—this one caught by Michael Missakian mooching a threaded anchovy.

We are hardly through admiring the fish when my buddy's rod bends double and he is onto a nice salmon. After a 10-minute battle, we have this fish in the boat, a 15-pound bright, shiny female.

The current has been carrying us toward shore, and we've drifted about half a mile from where we first put in. We notice many jellyfish in the water—large brown ones called sea nettles—up to a foot in diameter with long tentacles. Some of the lines are starting to hook up with them as we drift by. Their tentacles stick to the anchovies and the lines. Their stingers can hurt your hands. They also seem to put off salmon, which will not bite anchovies with jellyfish tentacles on them.

We move back to where we started, and again, we find the large flock of murres feeding on the anchovies. Our fish finder shows a school of bait fish about 15 feet below the surface. We stop the boat and put our lines in. It isn't 10 minutes until my rod tip goes tap, tap. I quickly pick up the rod and feel the salmon munching the anchovy. As the salmon starts to pull away, I reel in the slack, feel resistance, and quickly lift the tip, setting the hook. The salmon takes off in a run and line peels off the reel. After a 10-minute battle, we have a 12-pound salmon in the net and place it in the fish box.

Five minutes later Jon's rod starts to bend, and as he picks it up, a salmon jumps out of the water 50 feet from the boat. It's a smaller salmon but it's going crazy fighting and splashing. After it makes several more slashing surface runs and goes under the boat two or three times, we have this salmon in the net—an 8-pound female—bright and beautiful.

What a great day of fishing—the limit—two salmon for each of us. We give thanks to the sea that gave us this bounty and say a silent prayer to each of the salmon. We clean up the boat, stow our tackle, and start back to the dock.

On the way in, we clean the salmon. We examine the contents of their stomachs and find them full of anchovies. We carefully place the salmon under a damp burlap bag until we get in to the dock.

The seas are still flat-calm as we head back toward Point Bonita. The fog still hangs about 50 to

100 feet above the water, and we can see for long distances underneath it. As our boat cuts through the calm seas, we pass large flocks of murres feeding on the anchovies and pelicans diving into the bait balls. A herd of porpoise playfully accompany the boat for a few minutes, riding alongside and racing us before they disappear back into the ocean.

We round Point Bonita and see the north and south towers of the Golden Gate Bridge, its top still enclosed in fog. As

The day's bounty—three nice salmon on deck.

we move under the bridge, we burst out of the fog into bright sunshine. Ahead we see the skyline of San Francisco with its distinctive Transamerica pyramid.

The city looks very different from the water. We are almost alone out here, but we can see cars jammed bumper to bumper on the Golden Gate Bridge, and we can imagine all the offices with people working at their desks. We have been out since dawn in the wilderness next to this bustling metropolis. We have been in touch with nature. The sea, the birds, the fish, all the natural life we have experienced has renewed our spirit. We have renewed our sense of how we are but a part of the bigger scheme.

Now that we are close to home, our conversation changes to how we are going to fix the salmon. We decide to cut them into steaks about three-quarters of an inch thick and rub them with garlic, ginger, and soy sauce. Then we'll put them on a hot charcoal grill for about three minutes on the first side just to sear and mark the steaks. We'll turn them over and cook them for about five minutes on the other side, covering the barbecue for the last minute or two to give them a nice smoky flavor. The meat will turn opaque clear through and will be so juicy that it will melt in our mouths.

Chapter 2: Fishing Techniques For Salmon

"Salmon Fishermen Have 3-Pound Balls."
  – Quote from T-shirt

We launched Saturday, 10/25/97, out of China Basin at 5:30 a.m., on my 20-foot Grady White Wildcat, fishing with Debbie Moore, my first mate and co-captain, and Bob Kopernik. There was a breeze that gave us some concern that early in the morning, but it was from the east so we decided to head out and see. We went up to Duxbury and found the water very calm and fishable. After a couple of drifts in shallow water, we moved to a deeper area, 90 feet, and set up.

I was mooching 30 pulls down when the fish bit at 9:30 a.m. and I knew it was a large one when it took out a lot of line. (I use Calstar rods, custom wrapped at Yo's Custom Rods in Gardena, and Izorline.)

The battle lasted 45 minutes and the first time we saw it, it looked unbelievably huge, like two fish swimming together!

Bart Ribotta playing a small salmon hooked on a gitzit jig.

Debbie and Bob cleared the lines and deck and raised the motor. A hundred things can go wrong with a big fish, but they were experienced and took all the right steps. Bob was going to net it and kept the net low as we had seen a seal in the area.

Some boats saw the hook-up and were trolling pretty close but always seemed to be on the other side. Twice, Bob put the net in the water, but the fish was just beyond his reach and he wisely pulled back. Finally, the fish wore out and came to the boat on its side; Debbie got a great picture at the moment of truth. Bob got the net around it, and we hoisted it into the boat.

Our boat scale showed 52-54 pounds, but when we got back to the launch, we couldn't find a place to weigh it on a certified scale. Most stores have a scale that goes only to 50 pounds. The Marine Warehouse was closing, so we decided to keep the fish on ice until they opened the next day. Debbie and I went there in the morning and

used their scale. The fish officially weighed in at 52.20 pounds. The Marine Warehouse staff is experienced and very helpful, and they had all the information that the DFG needs (such as certification and witnesses).
—Bryan Dalton, "California State Record King Salmon Caught by Bryan Dalton" from Bay Area Regional Fishermen Webpage http://www.barfonline.com/RecordSalmon1.html. Reprinted by permission.

Trolling and mooching are the two ways to fish for salmon. In trolling, you pull baits or lures behind a moving boat. In mooching, you drift with the wind and current, and fish baits and lures over the side. Both methods will catch fish, but on any given day and in any given area, one will outperform the other.

Bait

To catch salmon, you need to understand how they feed. Salmon usually follow concentrations of bait fish—usually, anchovies, herring, or sardines—and send the smaller salmon slashing through the school, killing and wounding many of them. The wounded and dead bait fish gradually spin out of the ball and flutter or drift down to where the larger salmon are waiting to eat them. They leisurely mull them over in their mouths, turn them around, and swallow them head first. When mooching, you will often see your rod tip jiggling up and down for as long as a minute while the salmon plays with the bait. Don't try to set the hook and start playing the fish until it finally swallows the bait and moves away.

The most common bait is frozen anchovies (see photo above right), especially off San Francisco, where anchovies spawn in large numbers. But frozen herring hold together better in the water, so many commercial fishermen use them for trolling. In Washington and British Columbia, whole or "plug-cut" herring are often used for mooching.

Bryan Dalton holding the 52.2-pound state-record salmon. (Photo courtesy of Bryan Dalton.)

Frozen Bait

Anchovies and herring are the most common frozen bait, used after thawing. Anchovies are packaged in either bags or trays, and herring usually in trays. Bags contain 20 to 30 fish of various sizes. Some of the anchovies in bags are bent or damaged, but usually 90% are good. Tray baits are selected for both quality and size, ranging from 5 to 7 inches. Because no scales are missing and no fins are broken, tray bait can draw more strikes than bagged bait. But bagged bait is cheaper and contains fish of different sizes, which is often handy since salmon prefer different sizes of bait fish on different occasions. For example, if they are feeding on small "pinhead" anchovies, you can choose a small bait fish from the bag. In addition, bags often contain one or more sardines, which salmon sometimes prefer.

The scent of the bait

Salmon are said to have an incredible sense of smell, able to smell the water in the river where they were born. Salmon fishermen have many theories about how to get rid of human smell on their bait or lures. Some use rubber gloves so that their smell is not transferred to the bait, but this is extreme. My experience has been that human smell does not put off salmon.

Fishermen have many theories about how to help their bait catch salmon. One of the most popular is spitting on the bait or lure. Another is urinating on it, but this is a little extreme. Some people spray their bait or lure with WD-40, a lubricating oil, but seem to catch no more fish than the next person. I knew a commercial fisherman who soaked half of his bait in diesel fuel and left the other half clean. He claimed he caught more fish on the bait with diesel oil. Others who soak their bait in laundry detergent with bluing swear it catches more fish.

The bottom line is that the scent of your bait doesn't seem to make a lot of difference. What matters is that if you are concerned with such details, then you are probably tuned into the salmon and are going to catch more than your share.

Live Bait

Because salmon can usually be caught on frozen anchovies or herring, live bait is seldom used. But the added expense and hassle may be worthwhile if the fish are biting lightly, because salmon often attack a live anchovy more savagely than a dead one. (Fresh dead bait is also more effective than frozen bait.)

Once some friends of mine got a scoop of live bait and went south of San Francisco to try for the striped bass schooling off Thornton Beach. They backed their boat into the surf and started casting live bait where the fish were feeding. The four of them landed eight salmon, all over 20 pounds, and one halibut before they caught their limit of striped bass.

Live bait is irresistible when salmon and striped bass are both feeding on anchovies trapped in the surf line. Even though striped bass are generally fishermen's primary target in the surf, they're likely to catch a lot of salmon. To fish in the surf, back the boat just outside the last breaker. The engine should be running, and the boat should be out of gear. The bow must point into the swells, and the captain must be prepared to go forward if a big swell starts to break.

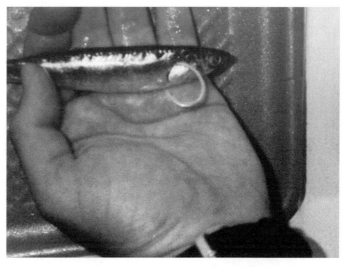

P 2-3 *A threaded anchovy rigged head down for mooching with a circle hook.*

Live bait is seasonally available at many of the landings listed in Chapter 6. Or you can catch your own. Bait rigs are the most economical method. They are available from many manufacturers—or you can tie your own—and usually contain 4 or 5 small jigs. If you lower a rig into a school of anchovies and jig it up and down, you should be able to get a dozen or more anchovies in a few minutes. More efficient and expensive (over $50) are cast nets. Casting them requires skill and practice, but you'll get all the bait you can use. When anchovies are tightly packed near the surface, you can use a long-handled brailing net to scoop them up.

Trolling

Trolling is an excellent way to locate salmon, especially when they are widely scattered. Not only do you cover lots of water, but you can also fish lines at several depths and try different baits and lures to find out what

P 2-4 *Frank Casey about to release a striped bass caught the same day as salmon on live bait off the Marin County coast.*

the salmon are feeding on. On days when you have no idea where the salmon are, trolling is the best way to find them. Of course, you shouldn't just troll blindly. Fish on both sides of current lines and tidal rips, passing periodically from one side to the other until you get a strike. Try to find birds and other signs of salmon (see Chapter 3 for more about signs). When fishing near groups of feeding birds or schools of bait, troll on their edges rather than charging through them. You don't want to spook them.

Running the Boat

Start trolling in a straight line, motoring several miles with and then against the swell. A typical speed is about 2 knots, although you can go slightly faster when using lures. If this approach doesn't work, try different speeds or patterns. Try changing speeds every quarter mile or so, because slowing down and speeding up causes the bait to rise and fall and attracts salmon. Or troll in a gentle half-mile-long S (see Diagram 2-1). The turns in an S-path cause the bait to change direction and speed.

When you get a hookup, slow the boat and steer in a gentle circle in the direction of the fish. To make fighting and

D2-1 An S-path for trolling causes the inside lures or bait to slow down and sink, while the outside lines speed up and rise. This movement will often entice salmon to bite.

D2-2 Starting a slow circle and playing the fish at a 45° angle to the boat allows you to fight the salmon without the boat pulling the fish and to net the salmon from the back corner of the boat.

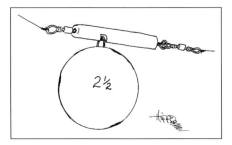

D2-3 2½-pound weight on a sinker release. The pull of a hooked salmon causes the weight to fall off so that the salmon can be played without the heavy weight.

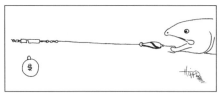

D2-4 A sinker falling off a release opened by the pull of a salmon.

Photo 2-7 Swivels prevent twisted lines while trolling. Sizes 7-2/0 are used for salmon.

D2-7 A diver on a line with a 4- to 6-foot leader.

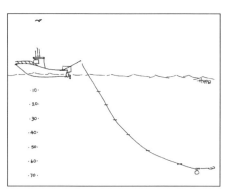

D2-5b To compensate for the forward motion of the boat, let out more feet of line than the depth that you will be fishing.

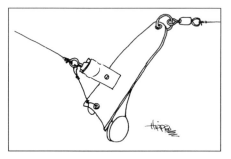

D2-6 A diver allows you to get the bait or lure down to the depth of the salmon (usually 20 to 40 feet). It also acts as an attractor.

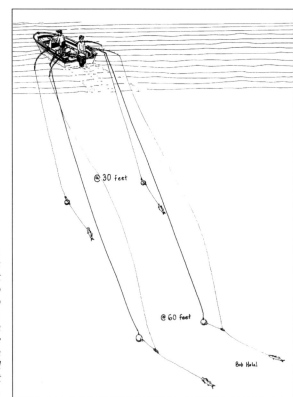

D2-5a A downrigger is used to carry bait or lures down to various depths up to 200 feet. When the salmon are located, the downrigger can be lowered precisely to that depth again.

netting the fish easier, try to maintain a 45° angle between the long axis of the boat and the fish (see Diagram 2-2). Leave the other lines in the water, since additional fish may strike. Once you bring a fish aboard, circle through the area several times before continuing on.

Getting Your Bait Down to the Fish

Because salmon rarely feed at the surface, you need to troll the baits down to the level of the fish. The three ways to do this are with a lead weight, a trolling plane, or a downrigger. Each one uses somewhat different tackle.

Weights

With weights, you can troll down to about 60 feet. Although small weights of 6 to 8 ounces will work if salmon are feeding near the surface, they rarely do. So most trolling is done with $2^1/_2$- to 3-pound lead balls (see Diagram 2-3). You attach the weight to a sinker release tied between the main line and the leader. When a fish strikes, the sinker will drop off and fall to the bottom, allowing you to play the fish without the weight of the sinker (see Diagram 2-4). Of course, with missed hook-ups, undersized fish, and landed fish, you can lose five or six sinkers, worth $10 to $20, in a day.

Photo 2-6 Trolling rods and reels. Rods are fairly stiff, and reels hold 150 to 200 yards of 20- to 30-pound-test line.

If you estimate the depth of the bait by counting the number of 1-foot "pulls" you let out, remember that a weight travels both down and away from the boat, so the number of pulls will be more than the actual depth of the bait. To get to the depth you want, you need to let out additional line (see Diagram 2-5).

Divers

With a diver, or trolling plane, you can fish down to about 50 feet without using a lead sinker. This device is attached between the main line and the leader and moves deeper as you release more line (see Diagrams 2-6, 2-7). Because divers exert a lot of drag, most have a tripping device that is triggered when a fish hits, partially detaching the diver from the line and decreasing its pull. Like weights, the depth of a diver is less than the number of "pulls" of line you let out. Unlike weights, divers aren't lost, and they can act as attractors—but you have to battle the weight of both the fish and the diver. Popular brands are Pink Lady and Deep Six.

Downriggers

Downriggers—reels with cables and weights that attach to your line—have dramatically changed salmon trolling (see Photo 2-5). They can carry unweighted lines down to 200 feet, a greater depth than is possible with weights or divers. Because the weights are attached to the downrigger line, you can use much lighter tackle. You can accurately set the depth of a downrigger, so you can consistently fish at the depth where you find the salmon. And you don't have to worry about losing an expensive weight every time you get a strike.

The technique for fishing with a downrigger is simple: Attach the line to a release clip on either the weight or the cable. Let out as much line as you want behind the clip, which will act as a leader (see Diagram 2-8). (I usually use 10 to 15 feet but have used as much as 30 feet and as little as 5 or 6 feet.) Lower the downrigger to the desired depth—on most downriggers there is a counter. When a salmon hits the bait or lure behind the downrigger, the line is released from the clip and you can fight the salmon on light tackle.

You can fish more than one rod—and fish at different depths—on a single downrigger by using "stacking." (see Diagram 2-9) You can attach one rod to a release clip at the weight and lower it to 50 feet, for example, and attach a second one to a release clip at the 30-foot mark and troll both behind the boat on a single downrigger cable. A strike on either rod causes the line to release, and you can play the salmon on that rod.

You can fish two separate baits at different depths on the same rod by using a slider (see Diagram 2-10). With a clip or a snap swivel, attach a 6-foot leader with a lure or bait to your line, which is already on the downrigger. The leader will slide down the line to half the depth and remain there until a fish strikes and gets hooked. Then it will slide down to the bottom and release both lures or baits; the upper one will have the fish.

Because salmon are attracted to movement, another good technique is to attach a flasher directly to the downrigger

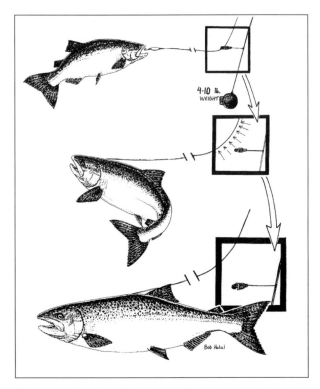

D2-8 A downrigger's line, release clip, weight, and cable. Weights are typically 4 to 10 pounds. Many types of releases work well.

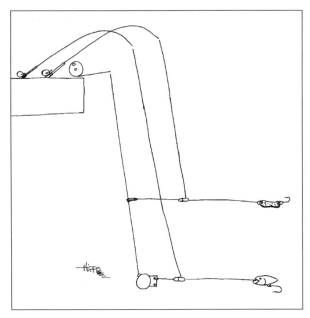

D2-9 To use more than one rod on a downrigger, stack the rods.

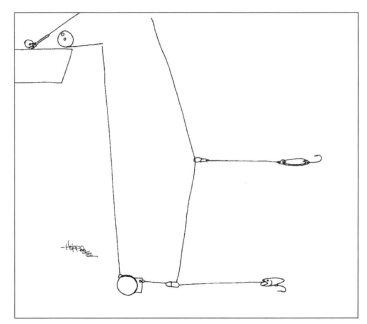

D2-10 A slider on a downrigger allows two baits or lures to be fished at different depths on the same line.

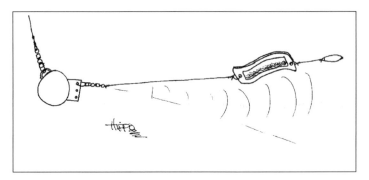

D2-11 A flasher on a downrigger weight acts as an attractor (a 6- to 8-ounce torpedo sinker keeps the flasher from spinning too much). Because the flasher is not attached to the line, the salmon can be played freely.

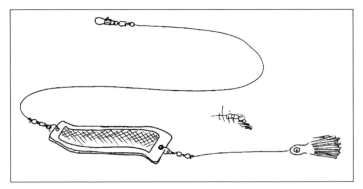

Diagram 2-12 A flasher and a hoochie, which imitates a squid. Use an 18- to 24-inch leader of 20- to 25-pound-test line.

weight to act as an attractor (see Diagram 2-11). A weight of 6 to 12 ounces on a 12- to 15-inch leader will give the flasher the right action. Attach the bait or lure several feet above the flasher. This arrangement gives you the attraction of a flasher without the hindrance of one when you play the fish.

Trolling Tackle

Rods and Reels

Trolling tackle depends on the method you use for lowering your bait. With a downrigger, you can use light tackle. With weights and divers, you need heavier tackle. Rods are medium to heavy, in the 25- to 30-pound class (that is, able to handle at least 25- to 30-pound–test lines; see Photo 2-7). Reels should also be heavier for trolling than for mooching, typically in the 3-0 class, although even heavier reels can be used, such as a Penn Senator 112 with 25- to 30-pound–test line.

Terminal Tackle

You can troll with either bait or lures or both. Start with a different one on each line and then switch to the whatever draws the most strikes. It pays to have a selection of lures on board. (See Photo 2-8 for examples of swivels and Photo 2-9 for an example of a spoon.)

Lures.

The most common lures for trolling are plugs and spoons in a variety of colors (see Photos 2-9, 2-10). Popular spoons are Krocodile, Apex, Point Defiance, and Andy Reeker. You can also use hoochies, or plastic squid, tied behind a metal flasher, which acts as an attractor (see Diagram 2-12).

Bait.

You can simply hook a bait, such as an anchovy, herring, or sardine, and troll it on a 5- to 6-foot leader. Thread a crowbar hook or e-z baiter through the bait so that it will slowly spin, imitating an injured bait fish (see Photo 2-11). Or use a colored plastic clip, marketed as a rotary salmon killer, to hold the bait and slowly spin (see Photo 2-12). (Later in this chapter are more details about selecting, rigging, and working bait.)

Photo 2-8 A salmon caught while trolling with a spoon.

Photo 2-9 Types of spoons for trolling. Left to right: Commercial, Point Defiance, Tuway, Crocodile, Andy Reeker.

Mooching

Mooching is fishing from a drifting boat, using either bait or lures. You simply shut off the engine and lower the lines over the side. What is the "correct" speed for mooching? As a rule, if the angle of the line over the side exceeds 45°, the boat is drifting too fast for mooching. To slow the boat, you can use a parachute or a sea anchor (see Diagram 2-13). (Twelve-foot parachutes are available at many surplus stores.) On the other hand, if the sea is dead calm and your lines are hanging straight down, try "motor-mooching." Start the boat, put it in gear, slowly move forward 15 to 20 yards, and then shut the engine down or put it in neutral. This action causes the bait to rise and then slowly flutter down, often attracting a salmon to bite. Besides giving action to your bait, motor-mooching also lets you cover a larger area than simply drifting.

Mooching has many advantages. First, it is more fun than trolling, because you can use lighter tackle. It can be more effective than trolling when salmon are feeding on large, concentrated schools of bait (see Diagram 2-14 for an illustration of mooching at a variety of depths). Mooching also allows you to fish in over 200 feet of water—deeper than you can troll, even with a downrigger. Mooching is also preferable when there are lots of jellyfish because a trolled bait or lure is

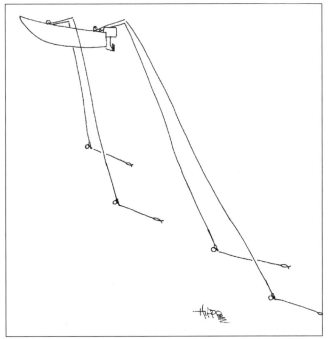

Diagram 2-14 Set mooching lines at different depths until you catch a salmon, then move all the lines to that depth.

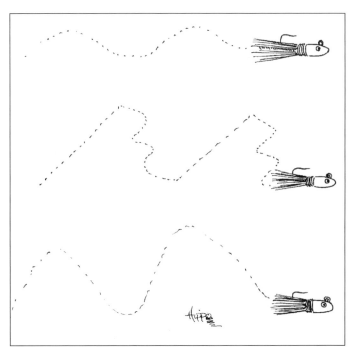

Diagram 2-16 The technique of jigging: try different patterns.

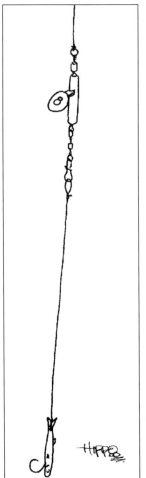

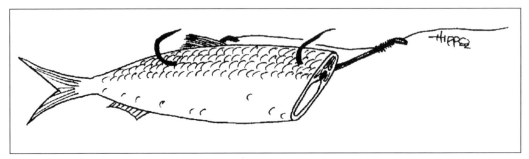

Diagram 2-17 Plug-cut bait slowly spins when raised and lowered, mimicking a wounded bait fish.

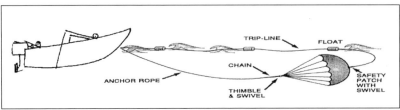

Diagram 2-13 A parachute can be used as a sea anchor to slow the speed of the drift caused by the wind. (Courtesy of Fiorentino Para Anchor, 1048 Irvine Ave. #489, Newport Beach, CA 92660).

Diagram 2-15 A trout-sinker release is used for mooching in deep water (up to 200 feet) with heavy (1 pound) weights.

Photo 2-13 Siwash hooks have a deep curve and are commonly used for salmon trolling in sizes 1/0 to 7/0.

guaranteed to snag jellyfish. When mooching, your baits hang straight down and drift at the same speed as the jellyfish, so you can often avoid them. The one limitation to mooching is weather conditions. Heavy wind, sea, swell, or current make drifting difficult, especially in a small boat. In these conditions, trolling, with its added control, is a better bet.

Mooching Tackle

Rods and Reels

Mooching rods range from a trout, or spinning, rod up through bass tackle and steelhead gear. Line size for salmon ranges from 6-pound to about 20-pound test; 10- to 15-pound test is the most popular. Mooching rods are typically 8 to 9 feet long with a sensitive tip to detect nibbles but enough backbone to beat 20-pound, or larger, salmon. A medium-heavy- to heavy-action rod rated for an 8- to 17-pound line is a good choice. A lighter rod takes more skill and a longer time to land a fish. A heavier rod lacks sensitivity of the tip. If you have to use a heavier rod, set it on a lighter drag so that the hook doesn't pull out before you can set it.

Your reel should hold at least 150 yards of the pound test line you are using. You need a smooth drag that can tolerate a powerful 50-yard run of a 20-pound, or larger, salmon. Major reel manufacturers—such as Penn, Ambassadeur/Garcia, and Shimano—all make good mooching reels. (Photo 2-14 shows a variety of mooching rods and reels.)

Photo 2-10 J-plugs for trolling. Years ago, these were very popular for large salmon.

Terminal Tackle

Bait.

As in trolling, the common bait used in mooching is frozen anchovies, herring, or sardines, depending on what the salmon are feeding on. (In the next section, you'll find a detailed discussion of different kinds of bait and how to rig and fish them.)

Photo 2-11 Hooked bait on crowbar for trolling. The bait should spin slowly to look like it is wounded. (Photo courtesy of Lon Tokunaga.)

Weights.

Light weights are used for mooching, usually 1 to 5 ounces, unless the current or wind is strong or you need to reach a greater depth. The common set-up is to tie a 1- to 5-ounce crescent, or banana-shaped, weight to the end of your line and clip on a 3- to 5-foot leader with the bait attached. Because banana weights do not slide on the line, they can give the bait a jerky motion, which sometimes entices salmon to bite.

Another popular way of rigging a weight is to clip it onto a sliding plastic sleeve, place a swivel beneath the sleeve, and attach the leader (see Photo 2-16). (I like 6- to

Photo 2-12 A rotary salmon killer is an easy way to rig salmon for trolling. It spins slowly, mimicking a wounded anchovy. (Photo courtesy of Lon Tokunaga.)

9-foot leaders, but many people like them shorter, even 3 feet). Conditions dictate the amount of lead; as little as half an ounce will work if it is dead calm and there is no current. If the current or wind is stronger or you are fishing deeper, go up to 5 or 6 ounces. The advantage of the slider is that when the salmon mouths the bait, it does not feel the weight because the line freely slides within the sleeve. But if you're not careful, a sinker on a sliding sleeve can get tangled in the landing net and you can lose the fish.

A third sinker alternative is to attach a weight to the line with a trout-sinker release (see Diagram 2-15). When a fish is hooked, the release engages and the sinker falls off. Trout-sinker releases are useful when the fish are deep enough to

Photo 2-17 A salmon caught on a jig by the author.

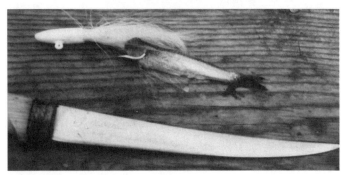

Photo 2-18: A filleted anchovy on a jig. The anchovy fillet adds smell and action to the jig. Regulations may prohibit use of bait without a circle hook.

Photo 2-14 Mooching rods and reels. Rods are long, 8 feet, and have medium to medium - heavy action. Reels have smooth drags and hold 150 to 200 yards of 10- to 20-pound-test line.

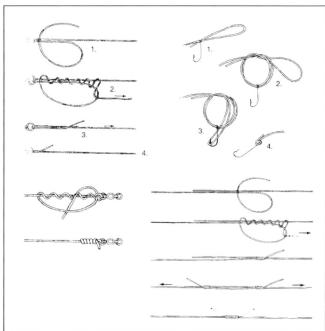

Diagram 2-18: Knots. Left to right: Uni Knot, Palomar Knot, Improved Clinch Knot, Uni Knot. (Courtesy of Izor line.)

require 1-pound balls, because the sinker falls off and you can freely play the fish.

Leaders.

Most fishermen use 20-pound-test leaders. I often use lighter ones—10-, 12-, or 15-pound test—because I think I get more takes. However, salmon are not usually leader shy, and heavier test leaders prevent loss of fish due to the razor sharp teeth of king salmon. Leader length is usually 3 to 5 feet, but I like 6 to 8 feet for two reasons. First, I cut the hook off and re-tie after each bait lost or fish landed, so my leader gets shorter during the day, usually ending up at 4 or 5 feet. Second, with a longer leader, the salmon can take the bait without feeling the weight as easily. However, a long leader makes netting a fish somewhat trickier, since you have to lead the fish to the net.

Mooching with Lures.

If the salmon are biting lightly and not returning, try lures. Salmon often attack artificial bait more savagely than natural bait. Mooching lures include metal spoons and plastic jigs that imitate fish (such as hair-raisers), squid, and worms (see Photo 2-17). Lures can be used alone but are often more effective when sweetened with a small piece of bait, such as a piece of squid or an anchovy fillet.

To prepare an anchovy fillet, run a sharp knife along the backbone from behind the gill plate to the tail and then cut down through the backbone to include the tail. The fillet should be 2 to 3 inches long and have a shiny skin side with bright scales. Hook it so that the skin side flutters and flashes and the tail hangs down to give an enticing movement to the jig (see Photo 2-18).

Lures may be fished with the rod in a holder until the salmon bites. But they work best when you hold the rod and twitch it periodically. Lower metal jigs to the bottom in sandy areas, quickly reel them up 15 to 20 feet, and then drop them again to the bottom (see Diagram 2-16). This movement imitates that of a sand eel, which salmon feed on in the North Pacific.

Because salmon will often attack a lure, you should, at the first sign of resistance or weight, quickly set the hook by sharply lifting the tip and simultaneously reeling as fast as you can to take out all slack and put a constant pressure on the fish. I use a much heavier drag pressure with lures than with bait, because if there is any slack, the salmon can throw a barbless lure.

Rigging the Bait

Circle hooks

Since 1997 circle hooks have been required for ocean salmon fishing in California from Point Conception in the south to Horse Mountain near Shelter Cove in the north (see Photo 2-19). The purpose of circle hooks is to make releasing under-sized salmon easier and safer.

Circle hooks go back thousands of years. Native Americans carved them out of bone and shell. Commercial fishermen use circle hooks in long-line fishing for halibut, cod, and tuna because they hook fish more efficiently. Sports fishermen have recently begun to use circle hooks for big tuna, because the circle hooks almost always hook the fish in the corner of the mouth so that the line doesn't fray or break on the tuna's sharp teeth. Circle hooks also allow the use of lighter lines, resulting in more hookups and more fish landed.

Circle hooks need to be fished patiently. Do not set the hook! Violent hook sets will almost always pull a circle hook out, even if the salmon has swallowed it. Allow the fish to take the bait and swim away. Simply reel until you feel resistance and then lift the rod. The circle hook will lodge in the corner of the salmon's mouth, and once hooked, it will almost always stay hooked.

Bait can be rigged in a number of ways. You can use a double-rig barbless hook or a single barbless hook; you can thread the leader line through the bait, or you can "plug cut" the bait. Because salmon often swallow their bait head first, bait hanging head down is often attractive to them. It also mimics how dead or wounded anchovies fall out of bait balls.

A double-rig hook is actually two hooks: one that slides up and down on the leader and another farther down. As of 1996, double hooks have to be tied so that they won't slide. Place the bottom hook through the tail and the second hook through the lower jaw and out the nose, or place the lower hook through the head and the second hook through the tail if you want to fish your bait upside down (see Photo 2-20).

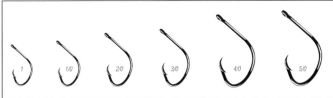

Photo 2-19: Circle hooks (barbless) are now required for mooching in many areas of California.

Photo 2-20: Double-rig hook techniques are popular for mooching in some areas. (Photo courtesy of Lon Tokunaga.)

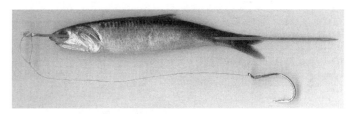

Photos 2-21 to 2-23: Steps of bait threading.
The anchovy is threaded backward onto the hook, using a bait threader (an 8- to 10-inch stainless steel needle pointed at one end and notched at the other). Insert the pointed end into the eye socket of the bait, being careful not to puncture the eye itself. Push the point through, to about half an inch from the tail. Attach the loop of the leader to the notched end of the threader and pull the loop all the way through the bait. Work the hook through the eye socket and finish off with a half-hitch around the tail. Slip a small rubber band over the head of the bait to keep the gills closed. (Photo courtesy of Lon Tokunaga.)

Another way to rig bait—an anchovy or, more often, a herring—with a double hook is to "plug cut" it. Cut the head off on a bias and then place a double hook through the head and the tail portion so that the bait hangs on the line with the head up (see Diagram 2-17). Raising plug-cut bait causes it to spin, and lowering it causes it to fall, movements that often entice salmon to strike. This technique is popular in Washington and British Columbia.

To use a single hook, place it through the jaw and out the nose so that the bait hangs head first. Or put the hook through the back, run the line along the side, and tie a half hitch over the tail so that the bait hangs upside down. You can also thread the leader line through the bait. This makes the line almost invisible, but it is time consuming. Insert a needle threader through the tail along the backbone and out the gill plate or through the eye. Attach the leader line to the notched end of the needle threader and pull it back through the path where it was inserted. Secure the hook onto the head of the leader and pull it down and bury it into the eye or inside the gill plate. Then exit the line through the tail so that the bait hangs upside down. (For bait-threading techniques, see Photos 2-21 to 23).

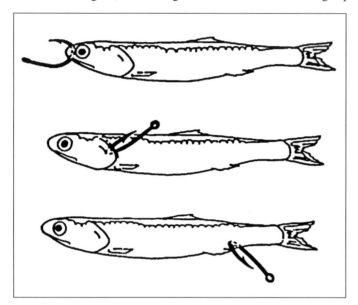

Diagram 2-19: Nose hooking. Put the hook through the bottom of the lower jaw, through the roof of the mouth, and out the top of the nose. Use this technique when there is a lot of current or drag on the bait or when it is necessary to have the bait away from the main line.

Diagram 2-20: Collar, or gill, hooking. Put the hook in through the front of the gill collar and out just in back of it. Use this technique when you want the bait to appear lively, especially with surface-feeding fish.

Diagram 2-21: Butt hooking. Put the hook in sideways just behind or directly above the anal fin. The hook should be perpendicular to the bait. Use this technique when you want the bait to dart out and down quickly and faster than a collar-hooked bait.

Knots.

It is important to become skilled at tying a couple of knots (see Diagram 2-18). These simple knots will be enough for most salmon-fishing situations.

How to rig live bait

Live anchovies, sardines, and herring can be hooked the following ways:

1. Nose hook. Put the hook through the bottom of the lower jaw and up through the roof of the mouth and out the top of the nose (see Diagram 2-19). The bait will "swim" naturally when nose hooked. Use a nose hook when there is a strong current or you are lowering and raising the bait.

2. Collar hook. Put the hook around of the tough gill collar from front to back (see Diagram 2-20). With a collar hook, the bait "swims" actively and flashes a lot as the line pulls it sideways. This is a good method when there is little current and the salmon are feeding actively.

3. Butt hook. Place the hook in one side and out the other just behind or directly above the anal fin (see Diagram 2-21). This method causes the bait to "swim" downward, which can give a good hookset because salmon swallow bait headfirst. Use this method when the salmon are deep.

Working the Bait

How you work bait depends on weather and sea conditions. If the swells are enough to make the boat to rise and fall and give action to the bait, you can simply lower it to a particular depth (usually 20 to 50 feet but sometimes shallower and often deeper) and hold the rod or place it in a holder until the tip starts twitching.

On flat, calm days, move the rod tip to increase the action of the bait. Slowly raise and then lower the tip 7 or 8 feet. To cover more of the water column, slowly lower the bait to 100 feet or more and then slowly reel it up, repeating the process over and over. Stay alert because salmon may hit either on the drop or the retrieve.

Experiment. If one technique isn't working, try another. Although stationary bait usually works, sometimes salmon want moving bait. Or try different baits. On one trip, we had both herring and anchovies aboard. Most people were using the anchovies and catching 6- to 7-pound fish. Then two guys tried the herring and promptly landed a pair of 20-pounders. Or try different depths. Remember, no two days of fishing are exactly alike.

Fishing live bait Live bait can be used either live or dead and fished the same as frozen bait in the open ocean. Live bait can also be saved and frozen and reused.

Setting the Hook

Some people wait until the rod tip gives a definite bend, but others grab the rod at the first tap and hold it until they feel resistance and can set the hook. Without a doubt, it is more exciting to hold the rod and feel the bite than to watch it in a rod holder, but this technique takes patience. If you set the hook while the salmon is still playing with the bait, you can pull it out of its mouth. Salmon are strong, soft-mouthed fish. Playing them on light mooching tackle requires finesse, not force, as is necessary with some other fish. A hard, violent hookset is more likely to lose a salmon than to hook it. In fact, salmon often hook themselves even when the rod is just sitting in the holder.

Salmon take the bait in two ways. They either immediately swallow it, or they play with it for a while. If the salmon immediately swallows the bait, your line may suddenly go limp while the salmon carries the sinker toward the surface, or your rod may suddenly bend and the line move off if the salmon begins to swim away with the bait. If your line goes limp, point the rod tip down, reel quickly until you feel the weight of the fish, and then set the hook with a firm lift. If the salmon begins to swim away, set the hook by firmly—but not violently—raising the tip in the direction opposite the run of the fish. (In either case, your rod will look like that in Photo 2-24.)

More often, though, salmon play with the bait, repeatedly mouthing and spitting it out. Your rod tip will jiggle, and you will feel short, gentle tugs. Do not set the hook right away. Wait until the fish swallows the bait and starts to move away. Sometimes this takes a minute or more; sometimes it never happens. But if the fish finally swallows the bait, set the hook by simultaneously raising the tip and reeling in until you feel resistance.

Hooking salmon with live bait. When you are using live bait, the first indication of a salmon will be the bait suddenly panicking. Wait until you feel the weight of the salmon before you set the hook. It may take a while for it to swallow the bait. If it doesn't, remember that bait that has been mouthed or killed will still catch fish, so it's worth lowering again.

Photo 2-24 The rod will bend when you hold it opposite the run of the fish, causing the fish to tire. (Photo courtesy of Bryan Dalton.)

Playing Your Salmon

Once you have hooked a salmon, apply smooth, steady pressure. Don't let any slack develop, because this will allow the fish to throw the hook, especially the barbless hooks required by law. With light mooching tackle, you can apply more pressure, since the extra strain will be absorbed by the rod instead of tearing the hook free.

A proper drag setting is crucial. You need enough drag to let line peel off when a salmon decides to run, but not so little that the line slips when you apply pressure. The surest way to lose a big salmon is to tighten the drag, because a powerful run will snap the line. King salmon seldom jump, but I have seen them jump 6 feet out of the water when hooked in the ocean. If they jump on light mooching tackle, you must bow to the

Photo 2-25 Playing a salmon with the rod tip up, leading the salmon toward the net. (Photo courtesy of Bryan Dalton.)

fish; otherwise, you risk breaking the line or throwing the hook. More common, however, is for a hooked king salmon to take off on a slashing run, breaking the surface several times. Then it will go down under the boat until you slowly bring it up. When it sees the boat, it will make another run. It will also make another run when its sees the net. If you miss the fish with the net, it will take off on a last-ditch run for its life.

A salmon should be played until it tires and lies on its side (see Photo 2-26). Then it is ready to be netted.

Netting Your Salmon

Salmon need to be played until they are fought out. Most salmon are lost if they are brought up to the net before they are tired and lying on their side. A salmon brought to the boat before it is tired or if it sees the net will inevitably turn and make a strong, quick run, often breaking the line if your drag is jerky or tight. When a salmon is tired, it will come to the surface easily. It can be directed with rod pressure into the net, which you should quickly raise, capturing the salmon and getting it into the box.

Netting a salmon takes some practice. If you are the one doing the netting, hold the bottom of the netting and grasp the handle in your left hand. With your right hand, grasp the handle near the end. Hang the net over the side of the boat close to the hull without touching the water (see Photo 2-27). Be careful that the hooked salmon does not see the net and

Photo 2-26: A salmon lying on its side, ready to be netted. (Photo courtesy of Bryan Dalton.)

become frightened. Thrust the net quickly under the salmon and lift it up. Pull the net toward the boat, keeping the rim above the water. When the net is next to the boat, point the handle directly upward and lift the salmon into the boat (see Photo 2-28). Do not lift the net with the handle parallel to the surface of the water because a heavy salmon will strain the handle and can bend or even break it.

Catch and Release

Although in recent years, silver (or coho) salmon have been rare and are seldom caught, in the past they made up a sizeable percentage of both the sport and commercial catch in California. It is now illegal to keep any silver salmon; they must all be released unharmed. It is important for every fisherman to tell the difference between king and silver salmon. The chart D2-23 shows how to tell king and silver salmon apart (make a photocopy and keep it in your boat). Your suspicion should be aroused if you catch a salmon that jumps, because kings seldom jump, but silvers are acrobats.

To preserve and maintain the salmon, sometimes you have to release the fish you hook. Laws limiting the seasons you can fish for salmon and the number and size you can catch and regulating the methods you can use are for the good of the salmon (see Chapter 4). If there were no regulations, salmon could be wiped out in a few years. For this reason, releasing salmon is an important skill to acquire. Undersize salmon as well as ones you want to release for some other reason must be treated with care. A successful release is a salmon that can survive to spawn.

Tips for Releasing Salmon

1. Handle the fish as little as possible, because touching it removes the protective slime and makes it suscep-

tible to infection.

2. To avoid damaging the scales or removing the protective slime, wet your hands before touching the fish.

3. Remove the hook with a pair of needle-nose pliers or a J-hook (see Diagram 2-22) while the fish is still in the water.

4. If the fish swallows the hook, cut the line as close to the hook as possible. The hook will rust out, and the fish will survive in most cases.

5. If the fish must be netted and measured, do it quickly. Don't let it flop around on the deck, and return it to the water as soon as you can.

6. Make sure the fish is revived before you release it. Hold it gently under water and move it back and forth so that water flows over its gills and revives it. The fish should be able to swim away under its own power.

7. Small fish and other fish that you want to release should be landed in as short a time as possible. A long fight stresses the fish and decreases its chances for survival.

8. Limit your catch. Kill only the fish that you can use. Leave the rest for another day.

A Final Word of Advice

No matter whether you troll or mooch, no matter what kind of boat you have, and no matter what tackle and bait you choose, the most important thing in catching fish is a positive fish attitude, or being confident that you are going to catch a fish. This attitude comes with understanding the habits of the fish and enjoying fishing. You have to think like a fish and be able to appreciate the ocean and all the different signs you see, which is the subject of the next chapter.

Photo 2-29 Frank Casey's small salmon about to be released.

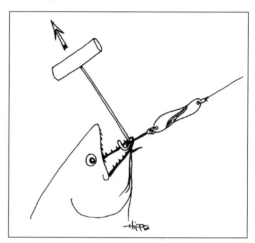

Diagram 2-22 Removing a hook with a J-hook. Slip the J-hook over the hook. Pull the line downward, causing the hook point to come out of the salmon's mouth.

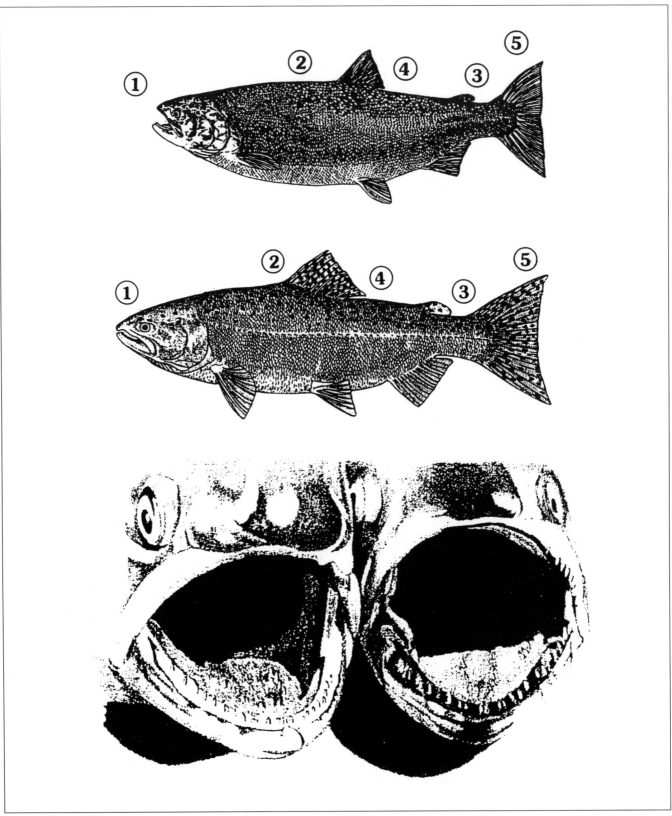

Diagram 2-23
TOP: *Coho (Silver) 1. Gums at base of teeth are white. 2. Small round spots on back. 3. Tail fin rays ribbed. 4. Color on back bluish green. 5. Spots on upper tail lobe only.*
MIDDLE: *Chinook (Salmon) 1. Gums at base of teeth are black. 2. Large uneven spots on back. 3. Tail fin rays smooth. 4. Color on back reflects purple in sun. 5. Spots on both tail lobes.*
BOTTOM: *Silver on left, has white gums around teeth, King on right, mouth is all dark.*

Chapter 3: Salmon Fishing from a Sailboat

Trolling with a Sailboat, 22 • Mooching with a Sailboat, 23 • Fishing While Cruising, 23

Photo 3-1 Fishing for salmon from a sailboat.

The salmon were running outside the channel buoys in 80 feet of water, and for the past week there had been good catches of mostly 8- to 10-pound fish. So we decided to go out on our sailboat. At 7 a.m. there would be a 4-knot outgoing tide, so we left the dock at 6 a.m. in order to catch the tide. A slight 5-knot breeze was blowing in through the gate, so we motored out at about 4 knots, which, when coupled with the outgoing tide, gave us 7 or 8 knots of speed. By the time we passed Point Bonita, the wind was blowing at 12-15 knots out of the northwest, so we raised the sails. The boat heeled over, and we shut off the engine. The quiet was broken only by the rush of water under the hull.

As we passed the last buoy, we saw the salmon fishing fleet about a mile in the distance. We approached and dropped the main and decided to troll using just the jib. We were making about 2 knots as we put in two trolling rods with 2-pound lead balls attached to sinker releases. We were fishing at 35 pulls when the port-side rod started singing as the fish pulled line off. Matt pinched into the wind to slow us down while we played the fish. After a 5-minute struggle, we netted a beautiful 8-pound salmon. An hour later we boated another about the *same size. Two more hours of trolling didn't produce another strike, so we decided to try mooching.*

We dropped the jib and started drifting. We switched to light-weight mooching setups with 15-pound test and 8-foot rods. Drifting anchovies with 1 ounce of weight down 35-40 pulls produced two more quick salmon, one 10 pounds and the other about 12 pounds. It was just past noon, and the afternoon northwest breeze had picked up to 20 knots.

We raised the sails and headed home with a following sea. Two hours later, after a great day of both fishing and sailing, we pulled into the dock at the San Francisco Marina. The reward would be salmon steaks on the grill tonight.

Although Monterey double-enders, the backbone of California's fishing fleet, were powered by sail, most modern sailboats are not designed to fish. Their small cockpits, exposed rudders, deep keels, stays, and boom pose challenges to fishing. They are dependent on the wind; under power, they are slow. So why fish from a sailboat? The number-one reason is that you have one.

But a sailboat has advantages too. It is the best way to combine sailing and fishing in the same trip. And sailboats, with their large heavy keels that resist being pushed by the wind, make good boats for drifting with the current and mooching.

Trolling with a Sailboat

Photo 3-2 Trolling from a sailboat.

How do you fish with a sailboat? Trolling is fairly simple, especially if you are under power. Troll no more than three rods—more is a problem. You need rod holders because trolling 2- or 3-pound sinkers will tire anyone's arms quickly. A rod holder can be as simple as 12 to 18 inches of 2-inch PVC pipe lashed to a stay or stanchion. Or you can buy rod holders and mount them on the deck, gunwale, or railing.

Trolling tackle for sailboats is the same as for any other boat. Use a sinker release or a diving plane to get the bait or lure down to the correct depth. Then use your motor to make 1-2 knots while pulling the baits and or lures behind. When you hook a fish, you must slow down but continue to make forward progress. Keeping the boat moving forward enables you to fight the salmon off the stern so that it does not go under the boat and tangle with the rudder. Turn the boat to keep the salmon off the stern at a 45° angle so that when it is tired and surfaces, you will be able to net it.

Trolling under sail presents more of a challenge and can be done only when the wind conditions are moderate. If there is no wind or only a slight one, you will not be able to troll predictably. If winds are too stiff, you will not be able to troll slowly enough (2 knots or less), even with only a jib. (I have caught salmon on spoons at speeds up to 5 knots, but landing a fish at that speed is a challenge.) Under favorable conditions, you'll usually need only the jib to go slowly enough. You can also reduce your speed by pinching into the wind. Reduce your speed this way when you hook a fish under sail.

When trolling from a sailboat, you need to observe a few cautions:

1. Coming about can create tangles, especially if more than one rod is being used (see Photo 3-3).

2. If you are under power, you can circle an area you suspect is holding fish, but if you are under sail, you need to make long, straight tacks.

3. When tacking with the wind, it is difficult to go slowly enough, so you may have to use power or sail back without your lines in the water and then tack back into the wind.

Mooching with a Sailboat

Mooching, or drifting, a popular and efficient method of catching salmon, is easy on a sailboat. When you arrive at the spot where you want to fish, just drop your sails or turn off the engine and put your lines in the water, or use a parachute to slow down (see Diagram 3-1). Usually the lines will be at an angle of less than 45°, depending on the wind and current. Make sure the lines on the side of the boat with the wind in your face do not go under the boat, or you will risk tangling with the keel or rudder and breaking off your salmon. When you are mooching, you can hold the rods or put them in holders. Because the boat is drifting, the bow is an excellent place to fish.

A long rod, 8 feet or more, is an advantage because you can control a hooked salmon and keep it away from the rudder or bowsprit. Long, flexible rods also give more action to your bait when you are mooching.

Fishing While Cruising

Usually, cruising is determined by the need to reach a destination within a given time. However, salmon fishing while cruising in a sailboat presents some additional challenges. Since salmon frequent the inshore areas, usually inside the 50-fathom line, most cruises need to make a detour to target salmon. Many good salmon areas are close to the beach, where rocky reefs can be navigational hazards.

Mooching for salmon means dropping the sails and drifting for hours, which can delay reaching your destination. Most trolling for salmon is very slow, about 1 to 2 knots, and this can create delays. If you are serious about fishing for salmon, you may have to troll around a specific small area where the salmon happen to be schooled all day. If you are able to spend all or a good part of the day trolling or mooching an area for salmon, that is the most consistent and productive method of putting salmon on your sailboat.

I have developed a compromise method of fast trolling, up to 5 knots, with spoons for salmon. This speed is often what you will make with light winds, and with more breeze you can simply reduce the amount of sail to lower your speed. When fast trolling with spoons, I use a heavier rod and reel, at least a 4/0 reel with 30-pound test line. I use either a sinker

Photo 3-3 A sailboat's rudder and keel can tangle lines when you are coming about when a fish runs under the boat.

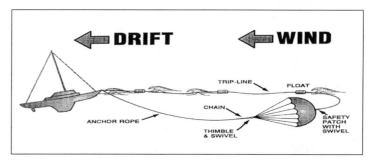

Diagram 3-1 A sailboat rigged with a parachute for mooching. (Diagram courtesy of Fiorentino Para Anchor.)

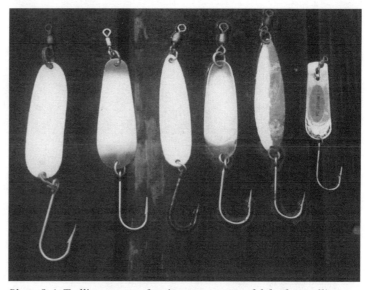

Photo 3-4 Trolling spoons of various types are useful for fast trolling while cruising.

release with a 3-pound lead ball or a large diving plane. Bait will not be very effective at fast speeds, so I use spoons, such as krocodiles (Photo 3-4 shows trolling spoons). Spoons have the advantage of staying fresh all day, but they should be periodically checked for debris, such as weeds or jellyfish tentacles. Spoons create good action at fast speeds, and salmon will attack a fast-moving spoon. Place a good swivel 2 or 3 feet up from the spoon to keep the line from twisting. Set the drag with the clicker on just tightly enough to prevent the line from going off the reel. When a salmon strikes the spoon, you will hear the reel singing as line peels off against the drag and clicker. Immediately slow the boat by heading into the wind while playing your salmon.

This method of fast trolling for salmon allows you to cruise the coastal waters and fish for salmon, without drastically delaying your arrival at your destination. However, don't just head up the coast; plan your cruise to pass by the traditional hotspots in each area (see Chapter 7 for these hotspots). Also look for signs (see Chapter 4), such as birds, bait, or current lines, and troll along these areas. Another tip is to look for commercial salmon trollers and troll where they are fishing. The commercial salmon fleet often fishes much deeper water farther offshore. Follow this advice and you will be eating salmon at your evening anchorage (see Photo 3-6).

Landing a salmon in a sailboat can cause a bloody mess, so have a large insulated ice chest on deck. Net the salmon and place it directly in the cooler while still in the net (see Photo 3-6). With a club, baseball bat, or hammer, deliver a quick blow to the head above the eyes to kill the salmon and stop it from thrashing around. Then take it out of the net and place it back in the cooler. Dip the net into the ocean to give it a good rinse. Using this method, the salmon can be landed with a minimum of mess to your boat.

Salmon fishing on a sailboat can be lots of fun. Each boat handles a little differently, so experiment—and enjoy the salmon you catch as well as the sail home.

Photo 3-5 A catamaran cruiser trolling for salmon off the Marin County coast.

Photo 3-6 A large salmon in the net. Since sailboats are usually high above the water, a long-handled net is necessary.

Photo 3-7 Matt Walker with a 30-pound salmon.

Chapter 4: Looking for Signs of Salmon

"The answer is blowing in the wind."
—Bob Dylan

Bait Fish, 25 • Birds, 25 • Whales, Porpoises, and Sea Lions, 29 • Sharks, 33 • Electronics, 34

Photo 4-1 Pelicans diving over the ocean are often a sign that salmon are pushing bait fish to the surface.

Greg and I were on the water by 8 a.m. Friday. His 23-foot Wellcraft headed for the Golden Gate Bridge at 25 knots. We were threading our way through swimmers, kayakers, and a myriad of sailboarders. The party boats were averaging a half a fish to the rod. So we decided to be opportunistic and look around a bit. We stopped to fish a flock of feeding birds just outside the Gate. Half an hour later, the meter still showed plenty of bait but not a bump for the boat. We pressed on. Cutting the corner around Point Bonita, we carved through the "popcorn" bumps, where the outgoing tide lumps up against the incoming waves. We stopped twice more on the way to Slide Ranch, 8 miles north of the Golden Gate Bridge. But with only a couple of tiny kingfish to show (they look like freshwater sheephead), we started to look about again. Greg paused a second to scope diving birds, then chuckled and throttled up again. He said, "It would be a rookie mistake to spend time fishing around those birds.

They're hovering over a sea lion that is tearing apart a salmon. There won't be many fish around."

Photo 4-2 Donald Forrest with a salmon caught near diving pelicans.

After we had spent hours chasing the fleet out to the channel and back, mooching with light tackle (1-ounce weight and an anchovy drifting at 20-40 feet) but with only a bump or two, the tide changed and wind whipped up the 5-foot swells to a light froth. We decided to pull the parachute that served as the sea anchor, keeping us drifting slowly enough to let the fish find us. As soon as Greg pulled the chute, his rod bent over the rail and cried in spurts as it paid out line in little bursts. I called, "Fish on your rod." He, like a good skipper, yelled back from the bow, "Take it!" In truth, I already had. I felt the rod throb in a strong rhythmic pulse. I envisioned a giant tail thrusting away with the hook. I sensed Greg coming around the corner and then saw my rod bend and whine. Greg had it in a flash and asked, "Do you want to trade?" "Naw," I said, "Let's just play these fish. We'll be lucky to land them both without getting fancy and worrying about whose rod is whose" In a second, we saw "color." True enough, a big fish. Strangely, every time, I heaved up to reel down, my rod in Greg's hand went limp. We gave each other a look that asked, "Could it be?" Too late! We looked at the 15-pounder thrashing on the top of the water—and at both our lines converging on a single 15-pound mouth. A double hook-up on a single fish!

—Donald Forrest

The first priority in salmon fishing is finding fish. On any day, salmon are found only in a small portion of the vast ocean. Although party boat and charter customers can rely on the expertise of their captains, the private boater must count on other resources.

Other fishermen are an extremely valuable source of information. You can often find out where the fish are biting by asking at bait shops or at the dock. (Phone hotlines and numbers of bait-and-tackle shops are listed in Chapter 7.) Listening to other boaters over the radio can also be invaluable. As one veteran party-boat skipper put it, "Hearing the right information over the radio can mean the difference between limits and getting skunked." The presence of other boats—especially boats catching fish—is also a good sign. Of course, you should always follow the rules of boating etiquette when joining another vessel.

However, relying on others only takes you so far. Salmon are highly migratory, and the spot that was red-hot yesterday may be fishless today. Some days no one knows where the fish are; other days those in the know won't tell. On such days, it's important to be able to read the ocean. With a little practice, anyone can recognize the clues that fish are present.

Bait fish, such as anchovies, can sometimes be seen jumping out of the water when salmon are feeding on them. At other times, bait fish ripple the water as they frantically swim underneath the surface .

Krill, small shrimp that swim in tight schools or balls, typically appear in the deeper offshore water almost every spring and are a favorite of salmon—and of whales and birds, as well. Krill can be located by gulls sitting on the water, dipping into the school. Krill can also be located by a reddish-brown color in the water.

Birds are the most important indication of bait fish and salmon—murres on the water diving for anchovies, pelicans diving into the water, or seagulls chasing bait fish driven to the surface. All these birds may be feeding on a school of bait that salmon are feeding on from below .

Slicks are another sign of bait fish on which salmon are feeding. A slick is a large area of water that is glassy-calm and shiny . Slicks can range in size from small, garage-sized areas to large expanses covering hundreds of square feet. They are formed by oil from injured bait fish rising to the surface. Some old-timers say they can smell salmon, but perhaps they are only smelling the fish oil from these slicks.

Another good place to fish is at a current line, where two currents meet. A line of debris or the intersection of two different colors of water indicate current lines. Current lines concentrate bait, which attracts salmon. Tidal rips also concentrate bait and salmon. These are areas where the tide hits a patch of still water or water moving in another direction. Look for breakers or areas with two different water heights.

The color of the ocean can also give valuable information because salmon often frequent dark water. Reddish water, such as the red tide that sometimes appears in the late fall, is a bad sign, since it is usually too warm for salmon. Light-colored water pushed out from the mouth of bays is also generally unproductive.

In the ocean, not only salmon but many forms of marine life are attracted to concentrations of food caused by upwellings, currents, or water temperature. As we will see, whales and porpoises are attracted to concentrations of bait fish or shrimp. Jellyfish are also attracted to these areas and can often be an indication that salmon are around. By-the-wind sailors, or sailors, are small jellyfish, not more than 2 inches in diameter, with a "sail" that sticks out of the water to catch the wind. Sea nettles are large brown jellies that slowly pulsate near the surface. Although sea nettles can be a sign of salmon, they make fishing difficult because their long tentacles foul fishing lines and cling to the bait. Salmon will not touch bait covered with stinging jellyfish tentacles.

In addition to all these natural signs, modern electronics are helpful in locating fish. A good fish finder, whether a flasher or a recorder (see the last section of this chapter), will show schools both of salmon and of bait fish. Whenever you find large concentrations of bait, especially if they are being pushed up from the bottom, you are likely to find salmon feeding on them from below.

Bait Fish

Diagram 4-1 Sea nettles often come in on currents that attract salmon.

Anchovies are the most important bait fish associated with salmon in California (Photo 4-8 shows bird over a school of anchovies). At times, however, herring, sardines, and juvenile rock cod provide food for salmon. They also feed on krill and squid.

Anchovies, herring, and sardines in California waters

Anchovies are a major source of food for salmon. Anchovies school off the California coast and migrate into the shallow water off the beaches during the summer to spawn. Anchovies are fished commercially for food, bait, and fish meal. Quotas are set based on Department of Fish and Game (DFG) biomass estimates. (Biomass is the fish population in 1000's of tons.) Biologists then allow a percentage to be harvested in order to prevent overfishing. The size of the anchovy quotas are controversial because the more anchovies, the more and healthier the population of salmon (and other fish) that feed on them.

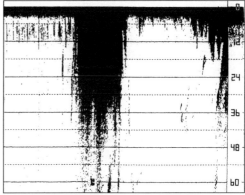

Photo 4-3 School of bait on a graph. Try to fish on the edge of the bait, not right on top of it.

Herring also school off the California coast, and salmon feed on them at times. Herring are fished commercially from Thanksgiving through March, when they spawn in San Francisco, Tomales, and Humboldt Bays. Commercial gill netters and seiners are allowed to take a yearly quota based on the DFG estimate of the biomass.

Sardines were once a major source of salmon food, and salmon from the Columbia River and even British Columbia would migrate a thousand miles south to feed on the huge schools off Monterey. Overfishing of sardines in the 1950's led to their near extinction and the collapse of the economy based on sardine canneries. Sardines have made a comeback in recent years, and the DFG has opened up commercial fishing with a quota based on the estimated biomass. Even with the commercial take, sardines are dramatically increasing in numbers and again becoming an important food source for salmon. The warmer waters brought by 1997-98's El Niño have been beneficial to the sardine population.

Birds

Probably the most important bird for salmon fishermen is the murre, the northern version of the penguin. It is the size of a small duck and has a slender, pointed bill. Its color is dark with a white underpart (see Photo 4-4). Murres often raft on the water or fly in lines. They are expert swimmers, able to dive down to 80 feet to catch a fish.

Murres have a symbiotic relationship with salmon. They swim over a school of salmon and stick their heads under the water to watch them. When the salmon chase anchovies or other bait fish toward the surface, the murres dive down and catch the bait fish. There is no better sign of salmon feeding below than a group of murres, some with wiggling anchovies in their mouths.

Photo 4-4 A drawing of a murre on the author's boat, the Blue Murre.

Photo 4-5 A pelican about to swallow an anchovy in its pouch.

Photo 4-6 A gull at Monterey.

If you hook a murre

Many times while mooching for salmon, I have hooked murres on live bait being fished on the bottom, in 80 feet of water. They look like cute little birds, but they need to be handled with respect when you are unhooking and releasing them. They have very sharp beaks, and if they bite your finger, they can leave a bad cut. Hold a murre gently behind the head as you unhook it or, if that is not possible, cut the hook or line as close to the bird as you can so that you can release it unharmed. Always remember that a hooked murre is a frightened wild bird that will bite you in self-defense if it can, and it can bite nearly through your finger.

Pelicans are the next most important bird sign of salmon (see Photo 4-9). Because pelicans dive to feed on bait fish driven to the surface, diving pelicans are an indication that game fish, usually salmon, are below. Brown pelicans, which frequent the shores off California, often fly in groups of five to ten, their wing tips almost hitting the water as they glide along the ocean swells. At other times, a lone pelican will fly over a ball of bait fish, fold its wings, and dive—with its bill, head, and body in a straight line like a spear—crashing into the water and then raising its pouch-like throat to gobble up a mouthful of anchovies.

Gulls are also important signs of salmon because, like pelicans and murres, they dive when salmon chase bait fish to the surface (see Photo 4-6). Gulls are also opportunists and frequently accompany pelicans to try to get the leftovers that the pelicans stun and miss.

Watch out for sea lions

One of the mistakes that novice fishermen often make is to run over to a place where a group of gulls are hovering and drop their lines in, thinking that the gulls' presence indicates bait fish and salmon below. But the gulls may be hovering over a sea lion that has caught a salmon, and they are trying to pick off the sea lion's leftovers (see Photo 4-7). Trying to fish in the vicinity of a sea lion is a big mistake because the sea lion will eat any fish you hook before you can get

it into the boat.

Other sea birds are attracted to concentrations of small fish but are not necessarily an indicator of salmon. For example, cormorants and grebes often swim on the surface over a large concentration of small fish—usually anchovies. But they are usually just attracted to the small fish, often in the shallow inshore waters, and are not especially associated with salmon . Likewise, terns, which are frequently seen in the Gulf of the Farallones, often dive for small fish on the surface, but they do not seem to be associated with large concentrations of salmon.

Shearwaters come to the Gulf of the Farallones in huge flocks in the summer, when the anchovies arrive. They fly around in circles, beating the water with their feet, and whipping it to a froth to catch the bait fish just below the surface. Another common bird in the Gulf of the Farallones is the petrel, a small bird that flits and dances over the sea, hanging its feet down toward the water. These small birds often accompany whales, appearing where the whale surfaces, most likely to pick up small scraps of fish that the whale provides.

Of the many kinds of birds I have seen in the Gulf of the Farallones, an osprey was one of the most unusual. Ospreys rarely fly over the ocean in California; they are usually found near rivers. But one flat, calm day when I was fishing off Duxbury Reef and the ocean was like glass, a gray and white osprey, or fish eagle, appeared, cruising over the ocean looking for a fish dinner. What a beautiful sight!

You may see other birds while fishing for salmon, such as ducks and black sea brants migrating north in the spring and south in the fall. Sometimes songbirds get lost out over the ocean, and they often try to land on boats or they flit around like they're afraid they won't make it back to land. Another flying species that fishermen see seasonally in California waters is the monarch butterfly. During their migrations to the Monterey and San Luis Obispo areas, they may fly tens of miles out to sea.

Photo 4-7 A sea lion eating a salmon, with gulls picking up the leftovers.

Whales, Porpoises, and Sea Lions

In the ocean, when currents, upwellings, or water temperature create a concentration of plankton or other food, you often will find whales, porpoises, and sea lions—as well as salmon.

Whales

The spout of a whale on the ocean is a beautiful sight. Whales, the ultimate symbol of wild nature, are the largest living mammals on earth. Because of upwellings of cold currents from the Continental Shelf, the waters of California support an abundance of the marine life that whales—and salmon—like to eat: krill (small, shrimp-like creatures) and anchovies. Where you find whales, you will usually find a rich source of food, and salmon will be nearby. Salmon fishermen always consider whales as a good sign.

Photo 4-8 Gulls and murres over a school of bait with salmon underneath.

The most common type of whale off the coast of San Francisco is the California gray whale, which reaches 35 to 50 feet in length and 20 to 40 tons in weight (see Photo 4-9). Gray whales migrate from Alaska to Baja California in Mexico, where they breed and calve. The trip is 6,000–7,000 miles each way and takes up to three months. They usually spend a considerable time feeding in the Gulf of the Farallones during their migrations north and south.

The other common whale is the humpback whale, which can reach 52 feet in length (see Photo 4-10). The present population is between 850 and 2,500 in the North Pacific. They often feed in the Gulf of the Farallones, even on anchovies (one of the favorite foods of salmon), especially during the late summer months. In the Farallones you may also occasionally see finbacks, which reach 76 feet, and blue whales, which can grow to 100 feet and weigh 100 tons.

Do not pursue a whale

Whales are thought of as friendly animals because they often come close to fishing boats and do not seem afraid. But sometimes, when approached, they run away as if frightened and stay miles away. We cannot forget that whales are wild animals. It is illegal to pursue a whale, and it can be dangerous to get too close.

Photo 4-9 A gray whale. (Courtesy of California Department of Fish and Game, Marine Mammals of California.)

Photo 4-10 A humpback whale. (Courtesy of California Department of Fish and Game, Marine Mammals of California.)

The Marine Mammal Protection Act, a federal law passed in 1972, makes it illegal for a citizen of the United States to harass a marine mammal. Harassment is defined as human activity that changes the behavior of the animals. Entering a sea lion rookery or closely pursuing a whale with a boat are violations of the act.

My friend Bart found out how dangerous it can be to get too close to a whale when he was fishing off Half Moon Bay in the summer of 1995. He and his friends had found a large school of salmon with several humpback whales in the vicinity. The fishing was excellent, and everyone on board had caught their limit. They continued to fish, doing what is called "catch and release"—releasing all the salmon they caught. While Bart was cleaning the salmon, he felt a bump, and the back end of his 21-foot, deep-V fiberglass Sea Ray was raised completely out of the water (Photo 4-11 shows Bart's boat). The boat shook up and down several times, knocking everyone to the deck. Several fishing rods bent double, and lines peeled off the reels. A huge splash of water came over the stern and soaked everyone. As they looked behind the boat, they saw the tail of a humpback whale splash as it moved away. This 40-foot whale had come up underneath the boat, caught its tail on the propeller and outdrive, and lifted a 2-ton boat out of the water like it was a cork. The whale had snagged itself on two of the fishing lines and did thousands of dollars of damage to the boat, bending the metal of the propeller and the outdrive and causing the boat to start leaking. Bart called for help, and a towboat was sent out to tow him in.

Photo 4-11 Bart Ribotta's Sea Ray.

Killer whales, or orcas, are rare visitors to the Gulf of the Farallones (see Photo 4-12). They are more common in the northern latitudes of Puget Sound and north, but they sometimes range as far south as the tip of Baja California. Recently, a large herd of killer whales was seen off the waters of San Francisco and Half Moon Bays. Interestingly, while the killer whales were around, the sea lions were absent.

A brief history of whales

The ancestors of these marine mammals at one time lived on land. Approximately 100 million years ago, they began evolving into aquatic forms and adapted to life in the sea. Cetaceans, as whales and dolphins are known, are streamlined to be able to move more easily through the water. They have layers of fat or blubber that insulate their bodies from the cold.

Commercial whaling reached its peak in the mid-nineteenth century. In 1840 these were about 750 whaling ships in the American fleet. After 1868, with the inventions of the explosive harpoon gun and the fast, steam-powered catcher boat and the use of floating factory ships, whales were quickly reduced in numbers.

In California, the first whaling station was established in Monterey in 1854. In 1886 there were five whaling stations, operated mostly by Portuguese fishermen. From 1940 to 1951, a modern shore whaling station operated in Eureka. In San Francisco Bay was the Richmond Whaling Station, which closed in 1971 because of federal laws prohibiting whaling. I remember going down to China Basin to look at the last catcher boat in 1972. It was for sale. A deadly harpoon cannon was mounted on its bow. It was a beautiful vessel, but it had bad vibes.

Photo 4-12 An orca whale. (Courtesy of California Department of Fish and Game, Marine Mammals of California.)

Whale populations were greatly depleted by commercial whaling, but many species are making comebacks. It is now estimated there about 11,000 gray whales, down from a pre-whaling population of 16,000. The future of whales lies with continued public pressure to make all of the international community stop commercial whaling. If we can protect and improve the ecology of the oceans, the future for whales looks bright.

Porpoises

The most common porpoise is the Pacific white-sided dolphin, which can reach 7 feet in length (see Photo 4-13). It feeds on anchovies and squid. It is common in the waters off the California coast. Porpoises do not remain in

Photo 4-13 A Pacific white-sided dolphin. (Courtesy of California Department of Fish and Game, Marine Mammals of California.)

one area long; they swim in groups, often following a boat for miles, playing in the wake.

Porpoises, like whales—and salmon—congregate around concentrations of food. Often when I am catching salmon, porpoises will visit, but more often, they seem to be attracted to the running boat and follow it for a while. Even though porpoises feed on anchovies, which are often used as bait for salmon, I have never heard of a porpoise being hooked on a rod and reel. They may be too smart and can recognize a hook and line and know that fishermen are trying to catch something.

Sea Lions

Both the California sea lion (see Photo 4-14) and the Stellar sea lion (see Photo 4-19) live in the waters off San Francisco. They can be seen at Seal Rock just south of the entrance to San Francisco Bay, and about 500 of them have taken up residency around Fisherman's Wharf (see Photo 4-16). The California sea lion, whose population is about 40,000, can weigh up to 500 pounds and measure 7 to 8 feet long. The Stellar sea lion is much larger, with males reaching 2,000 pounds and 13 feet, and females a little over 600 pounds and 9 feet in length. The Stellar sea lion population in California is estimated to be about 1,500 animals, with a large colony at the Farallon Islands. Unlike the smaller California sea lion, whose numbers are rapidly increasing, the Stellar sea lion is now on the federal government's threatened list and is being considered for the endangered-species list.

Sea lions get the big one

It was September and salmon fishing in the Bay Area had slowed down. The average was less than one fish per rod, but many of these were smokers over 30 pounds. It was a beautiful fall day on the ocean—calm seas and winds, with an overcast marine layer keeping out the sun. There were many boats fishing as we stopped about 2 miles short of Duxbury Buoy. After about ten minutes, I had a take that did not feel like a salmon, and when I brought it to the boat, I saw it was a large 15-inch mackerel. I kept it for possible use as bait, and put it in a 5-gallon bucket. Later that day, Frank hooked up to what he said felt like a nice fish. It made a long run, surfacing

50 yards out from the bow of the boat. Frank played the fish carefully, but after fifteen minutes he was still unable to gain any line. The fish was gradually taking out more. We were thinking about starting the engine and chasing the fish when Frank cranked down on the drag and the salmon turned and started a sideways run. Frank was then able to gain line, and the fish came toward the boat. As it got near, it made a run straight down under the

Photo 4-14 A California sea lion. (Courtesy of California Department of Fish and Game, Marine Mammals of California.)

Photo 4-15: A Stellar sea lion. (Courtesy of California Department of Fish and Game, Marine Mammals of California.)

Photo 4-16: California sea lions at San Francisco's Pier 39.

boat, and Frank skillfully worked the fish toward the surface. We could see its color and huge size as the salmon showed about five feet under the boat. It then made a runabout ten yards out and surfaced. The beautiful thirty-pound fish was just out of reach of the net. At the same time we saw a large sea lion 150 yards away rapidly porpoising toward our boat. I told Frank to tighten the drag and get the fish in quickly as I reached the net, but the fish made a last ditch run about ten yards down under the boat, and the sea lion was now only fifty yards away and closing fast. I grabbed the dead mackerel and threw it towards the sea lion in the hope that he would appreciate the free meal. The throw was perfect—the mackerel smacked the surface five feet in front of the sea lion—but he did not even slow down, and Frank's salmon took off on a long-drag, smoking run. After tearing off fifty yards of line, Frank finally turned the salmon. But a few seconds later, he felt a slow steady pull that he could not stop until the sea lion surfaced a hundred yards away with the largest salmon we had seen all year in its mouth. A couple of violent head shakes and Frank's severed line went slack. We were disappointed, but the sea lion belongs to nature, and nature's predators sometimes win.

Sea lions are the sworn enemy of salmon fishermen. Commercial fishermen, until the practice was outlawed in 1972, carried rifles and shot sea lions following their boats to pick off the large salmon they had hooked. These large salmon, in excess of 30 pounds, could mean close to $100 each in wages for the fishermen. It is not hard to understand why commercial fishermen see sea lions as their enemy. Sports fishermen who have had their lifetime trophy, 30-pound salmon eaten by a sea lion are no fans of the sea lion either. Imagine playing a salmon and all of a sudden your rod bends double and the line screams off the reel, as if the salmon has suddenly ballooned a hundredfold in size and strength. You look up and see a sea lion surface 100 yards behind the boat, shaking its head back and forth, holding a large salmon in its mouth. Helplessly, you watch as your prize salmon is lost to the sea lion.

But no matter how hard it is to lose a salmon to a sea lion, we have to realize that sea lions have been here a lot longer than we have and are part of nature, and we must share the salmon with the sea lions.

How to outsmart a sea lion

If I am visited by sea lions, I often move. This doesn't always work, though, because sea lions are smart and sometimes follow. But usually they will go to a fisherman closer to them rather than follow my boat.

I have lost many salmon to sea lions and have

landed a few salmon heads minus the body. Only once have I been successful in getting a salmon back from a sea lion. When it took a nice 20-pound salmon about 75 yards and suddenly appeared on the surface holding the fish in its jaws, we started up the boat and ran full speed ahead right at the sea lion. It dropped the salmon, which we were able to reel in, dead and minus its tail, but at least we got most of it.

It is not known how much damage sea lions actually do as predators of the salmon population. I have caught many salmon with scars on their sides that might have been the result of a sea lion attack, but I haven't ever seen a sea lion catch a salmon on its own in the open ocean. I have only seen sea lions eating salmon where people are fishing, and the sea lions seem to have stolen the salmon from the fishermen. Two stellar sea lions killed near the mouth of the Columbia River during a salmon run were found to have their stomachs filled with only lampreys. A study of 300 California sea lions' stomachs found the most common fish eaten was hake, which has little sport or commercial value. Sea lions' diet is mostly squid and octopus, supplemented by a variety of chiefly non-commercial fishes.

Sea lions often line up at the mouths of rivers that salmon travel up to spawn, such as the Russian River, about 50 miles north of San Francisco. When salmon enter a river from the ocean, they have to go through a narrow, shallow area where the river crosses the beach; here, they are easy prey for the sea lions. But even then, the strongest and fittest make it through to spawn, keeping the species strong and able to survive for generations.

Sharks

Sharks in California that are associated with salmon fishing are the great white shark, the blue shark, the thresher shark, and the dogfish shark. Great white sharks are common, and the other kinds are caught incidentally by salmon fishermen.

The great white shark breeds in the Gulf of the Farallones (see Photo 4-17), which is roughly formed by a triangle from Point Reyes (north of San Francisco) to the Farallon Islands (26 miles outside the Golden Gate Bridge) to Pedro Point (south of San Francisco). The abundance of sea lions in this area is a never-ending source of food for the great white shark. Another favorite food source is the elephant seal, often found near the Farallon Islands, Año Nuevo south of San Francisco, and in a new breeding colony at Point Reyes (in Marin County).

The great white shark, which can attain the length of over 20 feet and a weight of over 2 tons, is a powerful animal. It has been given a reputation as an indiscriminate killer by movies such as Jaws . Although sharks do occasionally attack surfers and skindivers, more often than not they spit them out. It is not known if sharks do not like the taste of humans or initially mistake them for sea lions. Deaths due to shark attacks are rare even though shark sightings are common off the California coast. I have seen maybe a dozen great white sharks, ranging from 10 feet to 20 feet. Great whites do not usually bother boats or fishermen.

A sea lion swam up to a 16-foot Boston Whaler off of Pedro Point and started to climb in. The two fishermen hit it with their gaff to keep it out. But the sea lion kept trying to get into the boat. They beat it with an oar, and it fell back in the water. But then it tried to climb into the boat again. As they were trying to push the sea lion out of the boat once more, a great white shark swam by. That sea lion had evidently decided to chance being beaten by two humans rather than being in the water with a great white shark.

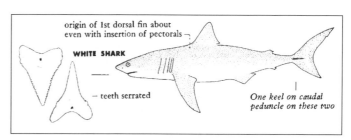

Photo 4-17: A great white shark. (Courtesy of California Department of Fish and Game, Guide to the Coastal Marine Fishes of California.)

Another salmon fisherman told me about an 18- to 20-foot great white shark that swam 20 or 30 feet past their boat. One of the fishermen beat on the water with a net to try to get the shark's attention. It turned around and scraped its back on the bottom of the 23-foot boat, causing it to rock and the fisherman to quiver with fear at the thought of the boat tipping over and their being in the water with a great white shark.

Blue sharks are caught while fishing for salmon (see Photo 4-18). In the Gulf of the Farallones, they range from about 3 feet to 10 feet in length. These long, slender sharks will often take a baited anchovy being used to catch salmon. When hooked, they tend to fight by rolling and spinning and wrapping themselves in the line. If you bring one up to the boat, it can cause a huge mess in your fishing line and leaders. Blue sharks should be released because their eating quality is poor. I have never seen nor heard of a blue shark attacking a salmon even while it was hooked on a line. However, I have seen blue sharks attack albacore tuna caught on a hook and bite them in half.

Thresher sharks, which weigh from 20 to 50 pounds and have a tail as long as their body, are also sometimes found around salmon (see Photo 4-19). Their favorite food is mackerel, and they are most often seen where there are a lot of mackerel. But they will also take anchovies being used for salmon bait and have been known to hit trolled lures. Thresher sharks can put on a spectacular fight, leaping out of the water and splashing their tail around. They are excellent eating.

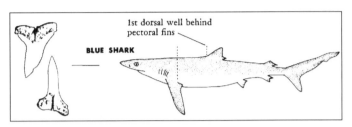

Photo 4-18: A blue shark. (Courtesy of California Department of Fish and Game, Guide to the Coastal Marine Fishes of California.)

Dogfish sharks are also caught by salmon fishermen—most often while mooching. These sharks are small, usually from 15 to 30 inches, and grab an anchovy and put on a twisting, wiggling fight. They should be released because they are poor food quality.

Many other species of sharks—such as leopard sharks and six-gill and seven-gill sharks—live in the salmon waters of California, but salmon fishermen rarely encounter them because most are bottom dwellers. These sharks are more frequently found inside the bay and go in and out with the tidal flow.

Electronics

Today, electronics are important additions to fishing. They can not only help you catch fish, but they are important safety aids to navigation. But keep electronics in perspective. Good fishermen still rely on reading the signs of nature, such as birds, concentrations of bait fish, and tide rips. Good mariners still rely on basic seamanship and navigation skills, such as the compass, dead reckoning, and weather reports.

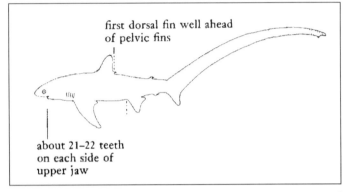

Photo 4-19: A thresher shark. (Courtesy of California Department of Fish and Game, Guide to the Coastal Marine Fishes of California.)

VHF Radios

The VHF (very high frequency) marine radio is one of the most important pieces of safety equipment that you can have on your boat . In addition to life jackets and flares, it can save your life in an emergency because the U.S. Coast Guard, marine police units, and towing services monitor distress frequencies. In addition the VHF radio provides communication with other fishermen, who can give you information not only about weather and sea condition but also about where the fish are, what are they biting, and how deep.

VHF radios operate on line of sight; that is, the signal is sent and received in a straight line (see Diagram 4-2). (Actually, the atmosphere can bend the radio waves slightly and add 15 to 20 percent more range.) Range is determined by the height of the antenna above the water and the "gain," or the equipment's ability to amplify signals. Due to the curvature of the earth, VHF radios generally have a range of 15 to 20 miles. The Federal Communications Commission limits VHF radios aboard recreational boats to a maximum power of 25 watts. Most units have a 1-watt standby setting.

VHF radios can be used to make telephone calls through the marine operator. However, MariTel, a telecommunications company, has a marine operator system throughout the United States. For as little as $25 a year and a per-minute charge of about $1, MariTel will place private calls from your VHF ship radio.

VHF radios range from just over $100 to $300. Some models under $200 are Standard, Uniden, Shakespeare, and Apelco. West Marine, a

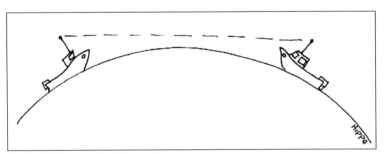

Diagram 4-2: VHF signals travel in line of sight.

popular marine-boat supply chain, also has its own brand.

CB Radios

CB, or citizen band, radios are used in addition to VHF radios, mainly for communication with other boats. The advantage is more privacy since they are not as popular. The disadvantage is also that they are less popular, because they have a smaller range and therefore are less dependable than VHF radios for calling for help in emergencies.

Cellular Telephones

Many boaters use cellular phones. They have 3 watts of power and, like VHF radios, are line of sight. Their main purpose is communication with friends and family ashore. They are not as dependable as VHF radios for emergencies because you might be outside a coverage area when at sea and cannot make calls through the marine operator.

GPS

GPS (Global Positioning System) is a satellite-based navigation system developed by the U.S. Department of Defense to provide a consistent, accurate method of simplifying navigation. Even though it was originally developed for military uses, it now provides commercial and recreational users with extremely accurate 24-hour, worldwide navigation information (see Diagram 4-3).

The GPS constellation is made up of 24

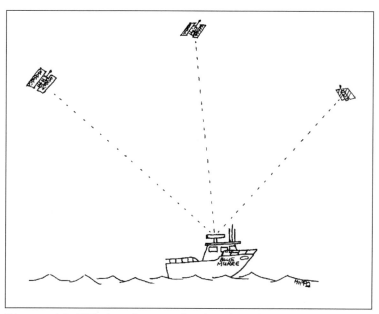

Diagram 4-3: GPS triangulates your boat's position from satellites.

satellites, which continuously send radio signals with their exact position and time back to earth. By knowing the position of any 3 or 4 of these satellites and calculating the time differences between the transmitted signals, a GPS unit automatically updates your position and tells you your speed and direction.

Because it provides accurate course and position information anywhere in the world, regardless of the weather or proximity to land, a GPS unit can make your boating and fishing more efficient and safer. It also allows you to mark the exact spot where you caught fish and accurately return to it. With a GPS, you can plot a route to any navigable spot in the world. Locations are marked by latitude and longitude (lat-lon) and can be read off any NOAA (National Oceanic and Atmospheric Administration) chart.

GPS units are relatively inexpensive, with many under $200, such as Garmin, Magellan, and Eagle. The price has been coming down, and some GPS units are now approaching $100.

Fish Finders

Fish finders register fishes' air bladders, so the term is actually a misnomer in salmon fishing, because salmon do not have air bladders. For salmon, fish finders are really fathometers. They bounce sound waves off the bottom and either show depth as a digital readout (a recorder in feet or fathoms) or as a flash beside numbers on a screen (a flasher). By showing the depth and bottom structure, fish finders can indicate where fish are likely to be (see Photo 4-20). They also can show schools of bait fish, and as a rule, salmon will be close by.

Fish finders can be purchased from around $100 for entry-level models to more than $1000 for the higher-level units. Hummingbird, Lowrance, Eagle, and West Marine all have units for around $200.

Radar

Radar is a good piece of safety navigational equipment, especially when fishing or running in heavy fog with limited visibility or in shipping lanes. Large ships travel at speeds of 20 knots and can't easily maneuver or stop. It is up to smaller boats to stay out of the way, and radar can identify these large vessels and help with navigation when visibility is restricted. However, most boats use GPS units for accurate navigation, because they are less expensive ($100-$500) than radar ($2,000-$5,000) and weigh much less.

Weather Radios

A cheap but useful piece of equipment is a marine weather radio. Radio Shack sells weather radios for $19.95, and other radios have marine weather channels. (For example, the Monterey NOAA broadcast is at 152 MHZ.) This radio can keep you in touch with the weather the night before your fishing trip and the morning before you leave. I have canceled many a trip by just listening to the morning weather report.

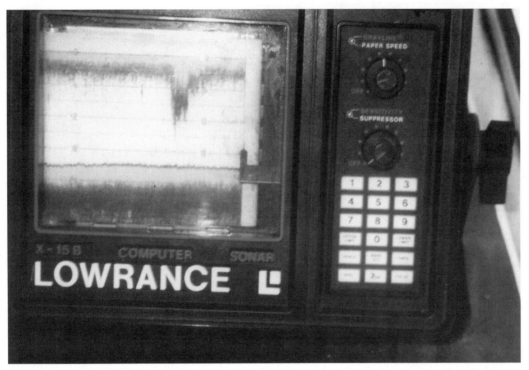

Photo 4-20: A fish finder is important to locate concentrations of bait as well as show you the bottom.

Chapter 5: Seamanship and Safety

Photo 5-1: Fishermen in Bart Ribotta's 21-foot, deep-V boat.

An increasing number of small-boat owners in California are enjoying salmon fishing on their own boat. Being your own captain and using your skills of navigation, seamanship, and finding fish is rewarding. You develop these skills with experience. You never stop learning.

Small and Very Small Craft

Boats used for salmon fishing in the ocean need to be seaworthy and, as a rule, should be at least 15 feet long with a deep-V bottom. Nevertheless, I have seen people fishing salmon from surfboards, kayaks, canoes, inflatables, and rowboats (for examples, see Photos 5-2, 5-3, 5-4 and 5-5). The number of days when conditions allow these very small craft to go safely onto the ocean are few, because they are not very mobile. They should risk the ocean only in sheltered areas or on very calm days. Some ports are better than others for very small boats—such as Shelter Cove, Trinidad, California City in San Francisco Bay, Half Moon Bay, and Monterey—and then only when the sea is calm and the salmon are close, within a mile or two of the launching area. But even in the best conditions, the ocean can change and conditions can deteriorate quickly. Always exercise caution.

Boats like 17-foot Boston Whalers are safe and very popular. Several manufacturers make seaworthy deep-V boats from 15 feet on up. I prefer a 20-foot or longer boat with a high freeboard for comfortable use on the open ocean. Many 20- to 25-foot deep-V boats come equipped with different types of engines: outboard, inboard/outdrive, or inboard. The kind you choose is a matter of personal preference and type of use.

Small boats can be used for both trolling and mooching (for examples, see Photos 5-6 and 5-7). Because small boats are light and do not displace a lot of water, they are susceptible to being blown by the wind. A parachute is often necessary to slow the drift. (See Chapter 2's discussion of mooching for information about how to use surplus-store parachutes as sea anchors.)

Photo 5-2: Fishing from a dinghy.

Photo 5-3: Fishing from a rowboat.

Photo 5-4: Fishing from an inflatable.

Photo 5-5: Fishing from a kayak.

Photo 5-6: A Boston Whaler.

Photo 5.7: A 23-foot Wellcraft, the author's boat, the Blue Murre.

Seamanship

Good seamanship and navigational skills are particularly important with small boats, because the frequent fog on the California coast limits visibility. Small boats are also more susceptible than larger ones to the dangers of swells, wind, waves, tides, and currents.

Tides

Tides are produced by the gravitational attractions of the moon and sun. Opposing these direct gravitational forces are the centrifugal forces of the earth's rotation, which produce a tide on the side of the earth away from the moon, resulting in two high tides. Tides vary during the month, depending on the phase of the moon: Full and new moons cause higher tides. Tides also vary during the year, depending on the closeness of the moon to the earth. Tides are measured in feet above or below mean high or low water.

Currents

The rise and fall of the tides, or flooding and ebbing, causes currents. The greater the difference between high and low tide, the faster the current. Between the flood (when the water is flowing toward the land) and ebb (when the water is flowing toward the sea), there is a period of no movement, called slack water.

Seas

Seas are waves or swells. Usually, they are created by

the wind far out on the ocean and travel toward shore. When they reach shallow water, they build in height. Seas are measured in height and frequency, both important measurements. For instance, a moderate, 5-foot sea every 20 seconds is gentle and hardly noticeable, but a 5-foot sea every 5 seconds is rough and unfishable. Wind waves are waves on top of the swells. For instance, there could be a 10-foot swell every 15 seconds, with 4-foot wind waves on top of them, making conditions very uncomfortable.

high tide	low tide	high tide	low tide
2 a.m.	6:39 a.m.	12:45 p.m.	19:20 p.m.
5.2 ft.	2.8 ft.	6.2 ft.	-0.8 ft.

Diagram 5-1: Tidal heights for Golden Gate Bridge, January 1, 1998

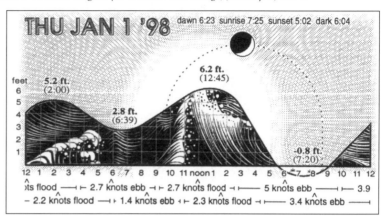

Diagram 5-2: Graph of tide for Golden Gate Bridge, January 1, 1998.

Wind

The wind can exert tremendous forces both on the waves and on your boat. It can make boating dangerous, because it can cause waves to form and swells to break. Photo 5-8 shows storm advisory flags.

Small boats and party boats

Party-boat skippers, most of whom own their boats, are a dying breed. They work hard, getting up at dark every morning, seven days a week during the salmon season, which goes from March to November and used to be even longer. They leave the dock around 6 a.m. and return about 3 p.m. Then they have to work more hours cleaning, fueling, and maintaining their boats. It is a hard life, but their freedom make them a unique group of people. They are a close knit group. You can hear them talking on the VHF radio. In fact, it is difficult for anyone else to use that channel. They are sometimes arrogant and unfriendly to outsiders, but generally they cooperate with the hundreds of small boats that compete with them for the fish (Photo 5-9 shows a small boat and a party boat at the edges of bait fish).

Much of the friction between small, private boats and party boats has to do with bad manners and lack of courtesy on the part of many small boats. I have seen small boats cut in front of a party boat, causing it to swerve to get out of the way. This can cause tangled lines and loss of a school of salmon that the party boat was working. I have seen small boats troll over a school of bait on the surface rather than off to the side, causing the bait and the salmon to sound and scatter, ruining the fishing for everyone. With the advent of party-boat mooching, I have seen small boats run full speed right by

max. flood	slack	max. flood	slack	max. flood	slack	max. flood	slack
00:10	03:41	05:56	09:16	11:58	14:42	18:06	21:52
4.0 knots		2.7 knots		2.7 knots		5.0 knots	

Diagram 5-3: Tidal currents for Golden Gate Bridge, January 1, 1998.

Seas	Wind Waves
0-3 feet = flat	0 feet, glass
2-4 feet=flat	1 foot, ripple
3-5 feet=average	2 feet, chop
4-6 feet=moderate	3 feet, uncomfortable
5-7 feet=moderate-heavy	4 feet, marginal
6-8 feet=heavy	5 feet, unfishable
7-9+ feet=dangerous	6+ feet, dangerous

Diagram 5-4: Seas and effects of wind waves.

Storm Advisories

	Small Craft	Gale	Storm	Hurricane
Daytime Signals				
Night Signals				
	Winds up to 38 mph	Winds 39 to 54 mph	Winds 55 to 73mph	Winds 74 mph and up

Photo 5-8: Storm-advisory flags. (Courtesy of State of California ABCs of the California Boating Law.)

a party boat that is stopped and fishing, causing the salmon to sound. Most of this friction could be eased if small boaters would show basic courtesy and respect. Party-boat skippers know what they are doing. They are professionals. We need each other. We have to be united. If we are divided, our efforts to save the salmon will be diminished.

Wind Speed	Conditions	Warnings
0-1 knots	glassy	
1-3 knots	ripple patches	
4-6 knots	ripples	
7-10 knots	small waves, less than 1 foot	
11-16 knots	longer waves, 1-3 feet	
17-21 knots	few whitecaps, 3-6 feet	
22-27 knots	overall whitecaps, 6-11 feet	
28-33 knots	whitecaps and swells, 11-17 feet	small craft advisory
34-40 knots	blown foam, higher waves	gale warning
41-47 knots		storm warning
over 63 knots		hurricane warning

Diagram 5-5: The effect of wind speed on waves.

Photo 5-9: A small boat and a party boat. Note that they both set up on the edge of the birds so as not to scatter the bait and the salmon.

Safety and First Aid

"An ounce of prevention is worth a pound of cure."

Salmon fishing is a sport performed in a natural environment that can be quite dangerous. The elements can be harsh, and accidents can happen. Some of the tackle used in fishing, such as hooks and knives, is sharp and can cause injuries if used improperly, and rough water can also cause accidents. Experienced fishermen prevent unnecessary problems by being prepared and thinking ahead.

First, you need a healthy respect for the weather. **Dress warmly and in layers.** Fishing in the summer off San Francisco can be very cold. The wind and the fog can sometimes create windchill factors down around freezing. A person in shirt sleeves out all day in this kind of weather can easily suffer hypothermia. A warm wool sweater as well as an outer jacket are standard gear.

Sunburn is another problem because the glare off the water intensifies the effect of the sun. Even on foggy days, you can get a sunburn. **Wear a good sunscreen** on all exposed parts when out fishing for a day and reapply it periodically.

Always wear a good pair of UV-protectant sunglasses when out on the ocean fishing. Being out all day in the glare of the sun can cause damage to your eyes. Sunglasses will not only protect your eyes from the sun but also from sharp objects, such as the tip of a pole, a gaff, or even a hook, that can come flying through the air.

A boat in the ocean can be a dangerous place. **Always have one hand holding onto something** when you move about the boat, especially in rough weather. If you are not holding on, you can be knocked down or even be knocked overboard. In rough weather, **wear a life jacket,** or PFD (personal flotation device). You should also have throwable life buoys or life cushions on board and practice man-overboard maneuvers so that everyone will know exactly what to do in an emergency.

Wear gloves when cleaning salmon. Gloves—whether rubber, cloth, or leather—will protect your hands from the salmon's sharp teeth and from slips of the knife blade. Cleaning salmon on a boat in rough weather or even on one just rocking back and forth can be a dangerous procedure. If you cut yourself when cleaning salmon, you can get a bad infection, called salmon poisoning, because salmon are covered with a slime that contains bacteria. When you hold a salmon by the mouth, its needle-like teeth can puncture your hand and cause razor-like cuts you don't feel until they become infected.

Try to avoid jellyfish stings. The tentacles have microscopic stingers that inject poison and cause a painful, stinging rash. When you remove jellyfish tentacles from your hook, line, and bait, some tentacles can stick to your hand. If you then inadvertently touch your face, they will cause a stinging rash, which is especially dangerous near your eyes. To treat jellyfish stings, wipe off the area with alcohol or an acidic liquid, such as vinegar or even tomato or lemon juice.

Treat hook injuries with care. There are two basic types of hook injuries. If the hook is buried just under the skin, it can be easily removed by pulling it out backward. But if the hook, especially one with a barb, is embedded too deeply to be easily removed, push it through the skin until the point comes out past the barb. Cut the barb off the hook with a pair of wire cutters. Then back the hook out along its entry path (see Photo 5-10 for how to remove a hook). Hook injuries, especially if contaminated with salmon slime or salmon blood, can easily become infected and need to be watched carefully. Allow the wound to bleed and squeeze it to make it bleed as much as possible. Then clean it with a disinfectant, such as alcohol, and wrap it and keep it clean. If infection or soreness persists, consult your doctor.

Plan ahead to prevent seasickness, or mal de mar. Either take Dramamine or place a Scopolamine patch behind your ear the night before your fishing trip. With Dramamine, take another dose just before you get on the boat. Scopolamine patches last for three days. Instead of medications, some people use wrist bands that put pressure on an acupuncture point, but these don't work for everyone. If you tend to get seasick, you should not go below deck, especially if you cannot see the water and are in an enclosed cabin. It is much better to be outside in the fresh air where you can keep your eyes on the horizon.

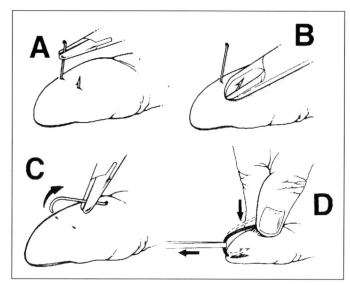

Diagram 5-6: How to remove a hook. A: Grab the hook with pliers and push the point through the skin. B: Snip off the point and barb. C: Back the hook out. D: Loop 12 to 18 inches of line around the hook. push the shank of the hook down with one hand and give a sharp yank with the other. The hook should pop out.

Falling overboard can lead to hypothermia. Even if you are quickly picked up and pulled back on the boat, the

---

Facts about seasickness

   1. CAUSES: the body's mechanism to maintain balance and orientation is also connected to fighting toxins, and motion on the sea fools the body into thinking it is poisoned.

   2. WHO: Women and children are more susceptible than men. People with high anxiety and introverted personalities are also more vulnerable.

   3. PREDISPOSING FACTORS: Fatigue, alcohol intake, or an unsettled emotional state can increase your susceptibility.

   4. PREVENTION: Sit in the middle of the boat where movement is less. Don't read. Try staring at the horizon. Get a good night's sleep.

   5. MEDICINES: Over-the-counter drugs Dramamine, Bonine, and Nauzene work. Prescription drugs, such as Scopolamine, the active ingredient in the Transderm Scop Patch, work very well.

   6. TREATMENT: Almost nothing, other than getting off the boat. The drugs work only if you take them before you get sick.

---

cold water of the Pacific Ocean (about 50° most of the summer) can quickly chill your body. In the water off the Northern California coast, people cannot survive for more than 45 minutes, and even a few minutes in the cold water can cause hypothermia. When you bring in someone who has fallen overboard, immediately remove their wet clothes, get them into dry ones, and wrap them in blankets. If the person is shivering and cannot get warm, the best way to combat hypothermia is for another person to get in under the blanket with no clothes on so that their body heat can warm up the person suffering from hypothermia. Hot drinks also help because they warm the inside. Alcohol is not good because it depresses the system.

A basic first-aid kit for salmon fishing should contain the following items:

1. Fresh water
2. Band-Aids
3. Gauze
4. A tube of Bacitracin ointment, a good antibiotic that will prevent salmon slime from infecting cuts and wounds
5. Adhesive tape
6. Vaseline
7. Sunscreen
8. Alcohol wipes

Store the items (except the water) in a small, waterproof container, such as Tupperware box. Periodically, make sure that the items are still usable.

Small-Boat Safety: 15-Point Plan

1. Have a trip plan and let someone know where you intend to go. If you do not return in a reasonable time, that person will know where to start looking.

2. Always go with a friend. He or she not only can help you find fish and provide company but also help if you get into trouble.

3. Check the weather. Listen to a weather radio at home the night and morning before your trip. If you don't, you may find you have to turn around after you get on the water. Do not go out when there is a small-craft advisory. Check wave size and frequency. Swells over 6 feet or waves over 3 feet more often than every 10 seconds require concern. Most small boat accidents are due to bad weather.

4. Check the drain plug before you launch. Many boats have sunk after launching because the drain plug was not in.

5. Check the bilge for water and gas fumes. Water can indicate a leak, and even a small amount of gasoline vapor can cause a deadly explosion.

6. Check the fuel and oil. The rule of thumb is 1/3 for the trip out, 1/3 for the trip back, and 1/3 for reserve in case conditions get bad and you need extra fuel to get back. There are no gas stations on the ocean. For the same reason, carry extra oil.

7. Have the proper number and type of life jackets (or Personal Flotation Devices, PFDs). It is common sense and required by law.

8. Carry drinking water. In an emergency, you will need water; dehydration is a real threat. You can go for days without food but not without water.

9. Carry distress flares. They are required by law and can be seen from long distances.

10. Dress warmly. Fog and wind can bring the chill factor down to around freezing; without insulation, you can suffer hypothermia. Dress in layers.

11. Have a working VHF radio. Get a radio check often, and make sure your radio is working before you leave the dock. Even the Coast Guard can't hear you if your radio is not working. A cellular phone is a good backup in case your radio goes out.

12. Have a working GPS or Loran. In fog, it is easy to get lost without one.

13. Carry charts, compass, and parallel ruler. If your electronic instruments fail, you need to know basic navigation to get home safely.

14. Know your boat's capabilities and do not exceed them.

15. Get towing insurance. For less than $100, you can have peace of mind.

On the next page, you'll find a checklist with these points and more. Photocopy it, laminate it on the back of the Salmon Identification page in Chapter 2, and go through it before you leave home to make sure you've remembered everything.

Boat Packing & Launching Checklist

In Boat:
❏ PFD's
❏ Oars/Paddles
❏ Depth Finder
❏ GPS
❏ Radio
❏ Rods
❏ Tackle Box - leaders
❏ Bait
❏ Down Riggers
❏ D/R Weights
❏ Net
❏ Waders
❏ Gunny Sacks
❏ First Aid Kit
❏ Tide Book
❏ Oil
❏ Plug In?
❏ Fuel

Personal:
❏ License/Card
❏ Sunglasses
❏ Hat
❏ Sunscreen
❏ Gloves
❏ Lunch
❏ Water
❏ Jacket
❏ Toilet Paper
❏ Watch
❏ Seasick Pills
❏ (Camera)
❏ (Binoculars)

At waters edge:
❏ Unplug Trailer Light
❏ Match PFD's to
   passengers
❏ Check Boat Plug
❏ Check Radio
❏ Bait

Planning:
The Night Before…
❏ Plan with guests
– times
– tides
– seasick pills

❏ *Emergency Contact*
phone number

Recreational:
❏ Red Flag
❏ Skis
❏ Wet Suits

Chapter 6: Care, Cleaning, and Cooking of Salmon

Photo 6-1: A salmon ready for cooking.

- Salmon meat is delicious.
- Treat salmon gently, because they bruise easily.
- Keep salmon icy cold until you cook it.
- King salmon can be prepared as fillets, steaks, roasts, cooked whole, smoked, cured, or salted.
- Salmon is not particularly bony, and bones can be pulled out of flesh with tweezers, pliers, or even fingers.
- Ocean salmon contains high levels of Omega-3 fatty acids, which play a role against heart disease.
- Salmon is high in protein and contains less than 200 calories per 3-ounce serving.

After Catching a Salmon

Salmon should be bled as soon as possible after you land them on the boat. Cut either the gills or one of the large arteries underneath the gills and hold the salmon over the side of the boat to let it bleed. Another way to bleed salmon is to clean the fish soon after it is landed. After I land a salmon, I club it on the head to stop it from thrashing around and quickly kill it. Then I remove the hook and place a large gaff through the gill and out the mouth. I lift the salmon over the side of the boat and insert a sharp knife under the gill and slit the throat, which causes the fish to bleed profusely. I hold it over the side for about a minute and then rinse it off and place it in the fish box.

Salmon should be kept cool. One of the easiest ways is to place it on a wet burlap sack on a rack in a ventilated fish box so that it does not sit in water. Then cover the fish with another wet burlap sack. The evaporation of the water from the burlap keeps the fish cool. To keep the fish out of direct sun, place a lid over the fish box. Most days off the Northern California coast, temperatures are in the 50s, so wet burlap sacks are enough to keep the salmon cool. To keep the meat fresh on a rare hot day, place the fish on ice in a large insulated cooler or an insulated box immediately after catching it.

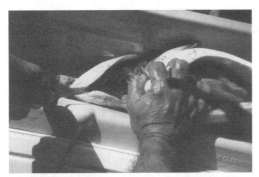

Photo 6-2: Cleaning salmon. Step 1: Detach the gills.

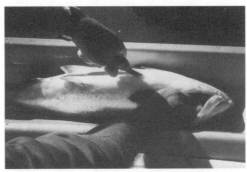

Photo 6-3: Cleaning salmon. Step 2: Slit the belly.

Cleaning Salmon

Salmon should be kept cool after they are landed and cleaned by the end of a day of fishing. A large V-shaped trough is convenient for cleaning the fish. You can make a trough of wood or buy a fiberglass one. Place the salmon in the trough with the back down and the stomach up. The first step is to detach the gills (see Photo 6-2). Insert a sharp fillet knife under one gill and cut from the top of the head. Then slide the knife around the gill, slicing the membrane that

Photo 6-4: Cleaning salmon. Step 3: Lift out the entrails.

Photo 6-5: Cleaning salmon. Step 4: Remove the bloodline.

holds the gill to the collar and cut through the gills attached to the lower jaw. Turn the salmon over and detach the other gill in the same way. Next, make a slit through the belly from behind the ventral fin almost up to the throat, leaving a small piece of flesh intact (see Photo 6-3). Slide in your hand, grabbing the gills, to lift out the entrails—stomach and intestines, liver, and testes or eggs—in one piece (see Photo 6-4). The next step is to remove the bloodline just in front of the backbone (see Photo 6-5). It is an area of dark reddish brown tissue covered with a thin membrane. Cut through the membrane with the sharp end of the knife to expose the bloodline. Then use a spoon or the spoon-shaped attachment on the handle of your knife to scrape out the bloodline. Then rinse the salmon of all blood and mucus and place it on a wet burlap sack or in an ice chest.

Salmon can be scaled simply by hosing them off with a jet of water from the tail toward the head. But do not scale fish that are not going to be eaten right away, especially if they are going to be frozen. The scales and skin protect meat that it is being frozen.

Cutting Up Salmon

Butcher the salmon for the way you want to cook it. Salmon can be cooked whole, steaked, filleted, or cut in chunks (recipes appear at the end of this chapter). The size of the fish to some extent determines how you should cook it. For instance, a small salmon should probably not be steaked or filleted because the steaks or fillets would be too small. It is better to cook a small a small salmon whole or in chunks. A large fish, on the other hand, is difficult to cook whole because it is thick in the mid-section and thin at the tail. To steak a large fish, cut the steak in half because a steak from a 20-pound salmon will take up a whole plate. Or fillet a large salmon and then cut the fillets into serving-sized steaks.

Whole Salmon

Preparing a salmon to be eaten whole is fairly simple. First, select a small to medium salmon. Cut off the head, if necessary, so that it will fit in the pan (see Photo 6-6). If the salmon is very small, keep the head on as decoration and for the good meat in the cheeks and collar. Likewise, cut off the tail or leave it on—it often turns crisp when baked and is a delicacy, almost like eating potato chips. Salmon in the 4- to 6-pound range can be either poached or baked whole. Salmon in the 6- to 8-pound range can be baked whole or stuffed and baked. Larger salmon can also be baked, but baking them whole is less satisfactory because the thickest part will not get done and the thinnest part will be dry and overdone.

Steaking Salmon

Steaking is one of the easiest and most popular ways of preparing salmon. To steak a salmon, cut off the head, lay the body on a cutting board on its side and with a sharp knife, cut steaks about 3/4 to 1 inch thick, cutting perpendicular to the backbone (see Photo 6-7). Cutting down to the backbone is fairly easy. Getting through the backbone is a little more difficult, and some experience is necessary. Move the knife back and forth to try to find the joint between the vertebrae so that the knife can go through easily. First, try in one spot, pushing on the backbone. If the knife does not go through easily, then move the blade slightly up or down the backbone to find the soft spot between the vertebrae. It will still take a little force to get through the vertebrae. But do not use too much force or you will mash the salmon meat beneath the vertebrae on the other side. Once you cut through the vertebrae, it is easy to continue cutting the rest of the way through the other side. What comes off is a beautiful, red, oval salmon steak. On a small fish, these steaks may be only half of a portion; on a very large fish, one steak may serve two or three people. When cutting large steaks in half, removing the backbone is simple. Salmon steaks can be cooked in almost any method—fried, baked, broiled, barbecued, pouched, or sautéed.

Photo 6-6: A whole salmon with the head cut off. (Photo courtesy of Michael Missakian.)

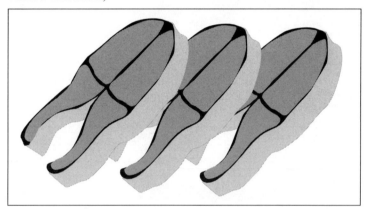

Photo 6-7: Steaking a salmon.

Filleting Salmon

Filleting a salmon is another good way to prepare the meat. To fillet a salmon, lay it on its side and, with a sharp knife, cut along the dorsal fin toward the backbone (see Photo 6-8). A row of bones goes all the way down the middle of the salmon's back in line with the dorsal fin from head to tail . Using these bones as a guide, slide the fillet knife down to the backbone and cut from head to tail. Then lift up the dorsal part of the fillet and use the pointed end of the knife to gently fillet around the backbone, which comes up in a rounded portion about the size of your thumb, and gently fillet the meat off the backbone. Once the backbone has been filleted, it is quite simple to fillet off the belly half of the meat. Use the rib

Photo 6-8: Salmon fillets. (Photo courtesy of Michael Missakian.)

bones down the midline of the fish as a guide, as well as the bones in the tail section. When this cut is complete, you will have a fillet that consists of half of the meat of the salmon. Turn the salmon over and repeat the same procedure on the other side so that you have two pieces of meat, each containing half the meat on the salmon. Leave the skin on because it prevents drying during cooking and holds the fillet together. The next step is to cut the fillets into serving-sized pieces. A small fillet cut in thirds will provide three servings per side. A large fillet may need to be cut into steaks about 1 inch thick, which are essentially the equivalent of half a steak without the backbone. Fillets can also be cut into half steaks and then into cubes for stir frying or shish-kabob.

Storing Salmon

If you catch more salmon than you can eat that day, there are a number of ways to keep it. Salmon can be refrigerated for two or three days or frozen for a month or two. To preserve it longer, it can be salted, smoked, turned into jerky, canned, or pickled.

Refrigeration and Freezing

Keeping salmon takes some care. Salmon, cut in any size, will stay good in the refrigerator for two to three days. If you are not going to eat the salmon within three days, freeze it and then thaw it out in the refrigerator. Some commercial fisherman quickly clean their salmon, freeze them, and then sell them to restaurants, which claim the quality of quick-frozen fish is better than that of fresh fish. I believe this may, in fact, be true. Most store-bought "fresh" salmon is actually seven to ten days old. The average commercial salmon trip is seven to ten days, so that fish caught at the beginning of the trip are cleaned and iced down for a week or more. Then it takes a day for a salmon boat to unload and get the fish to a wholesaler. Then it takes another day before this salmon gets to the market.

Freeze salmon as soon as you get home except for that which you are going to eat in the next couple of days. Be

realistic. Salmon is a very rich fish. Many times, I have said to my family, "Look at all the salmon I got." I'm thinking we'll eat salmon every day for the next three or four days. But after two days, we don't want to eat it again. There are several ways to freeze salmon. Leave on as much skin as possible because it protects the meat from air, preventing freezer burn and keeping the meat fresh. The best part to freeze is the tail section, where the skin entirely covers the fish except for the cut surface. Wrap the salmon tightly with freezer paper or heavy foil to prevent air from getting to the meat. Another way to freeze salmon is to place the amount you want to freeze, usually one to four servings, into a zip-lock bag. Add water and squeeze out all the air and then zip up the bag so there is no air, just water. Or immerse the open bag containing the fish in a large bowl or container filled with water. The water pressure will push against the bag and squeeze all the air out. The air will bubble to the surface, and when you close the zip-lock bag under water, there will be no air in it.

Photo 6-9: Smoked salmon. (Photo courtesy of Michael Missakian.)

Even under the best conditions, frozen salmon starts to lose quality after a month or two. Frozen salmon should be thawed in the refrigerator for a day because thawing it too quickly causes the cells to break down and lose moisture.

Salting

Salting salmon is another way of preserving it. Fillet the salmon, cut it into 4- to 6-inch long chunks, and pack them in salt. Start with a layer of salt, then a layer of meat, and so on. Salted salmon can be preserved for many months.

To use salted salmon, soak it in water for several hours or overnight to rinse out the salt. You can cook the salmon after rinsing it, but salted salmon is usually much better in soups or added to another dish. Salted salmon is used in the Hawaiian salad, lomi-lomi—made of small pieces of salmon and tomatoes (see Recipe 15 at the end of this chapter).

Smoking

Smoking salmon is an excellent way to preserve salmon (see Photo 6-9). Salmon can be smoked cold or hot.

Lox is cold-smoked salmon. The salmon is filleted and soaked for 6 to 8 hours or overnight in a brine solution of 1 cup salt to 1 quart of water, and then hung to dry. It is smoked for one or more days with cold smoke (no

Photo 6-10: Smoker. (Photo courtesy of Michael Missakian.)

heat, just the smoke that is far enough from the fish that it is cold).

In hot smoking (also called Indian-cured or Indian-smoked), the salmon is smoked over a hot fire to cook it and give it a smoky flavor.

To smoke salmon Indian style, soak fillets in a brine solution of 1 cup of sugar, 1 cup of salt, and 1 cup of water for 6 to 8 hours; spices, such as juniper berries, wine or various herbs, can be added to the brine solution. Take fillets out of the brine and dry them on a rack until a skin forms on the meat. Place dried fillets in a smoker and smoke them for 8 to 10 hours or until slightly moist.

You can buy an inexpensive smoker (a box with racks and an electric hot plate at the bottom) at a sporting goods store, or you can make your own in a 55-gallon drum, an old refrigerator, or any enclosed container (see Photo 6-10). Set wood shavings and wood chips in a pan on top of an electric hot plate so that they smolder to smoke the salmon. (Different kinds of wood give different flavors to the fish; hickory, oak, madrone, and alder are popular.) The hot plate makes enough smoke from the wood shavings to cook the salmon. Smokers need to be watched closely, and wood chips need to be added every couple of hours.

Salmon Jerky

To make jerky, cut salmon fillets the long way into strips half an inch by 1 inch. In a hot, dry climate, you can dry the strips in the sun. In a cool, moist climate, make jerky in the oven. Lay the salmon strips on a rack in a 200° oven and bake for several hours until they are dried. Salmon jerky is a nutritious and tasty snack.

Canned Salmon

Canning salmon is fairly easy. Put either filleted or chunked salmon in pint mason jars. Place the jars in a pressure cooker and cook them for 11/2 hours at 15 PSI with the tops slightly screwed on. Vent the pressure cooker. Then tighten the tops and allow the jars to cool.

Pickled Salmon

Pickling salmon takes time, but it will stay good for a year, at least. Cut 3-4 pounds of skinned fillets into bite-size pieces and place in a salt brine of 4 cups of water and 1 cup of pickling salt. Cover and refrigerate for 48 hours. Rinse fish thoroughly with cold water and drain. Cover salmon chunks with white vinegar and refrigerate for 24 hours. Drain the vinegar and place the fish in jars with layers of sliced onions and the following pickling solution:

Mix 2 cups of white vinegar, 1 to 11/2 cups of white sugar, 4 bay leaves, 5 or more whole cloves (or 6 cardamom seeds), 1 teaspoon mustard seed, and 1 teaspoon whole black pepper. Bring mixture to a boil, and cool before adding to jars. Refrigerate for 2 weeks before eating. If kept refrigerated, pickled fish should remain good for at least a year. (Recipe courtesy of Chauncey Hanson.)

Raw Salmon (Sushi and Sashimi)

Salmon is not eaten raw as sushi and sashimi by traditional Japanese due to the possibility of parasites. Trained sushi chefs freeze, smoke, or salt salmon for sushi. However, with the popularity of sushi, some restaurants serve raw salmon. You should eat raw salmon sushi only if you are willing to take the risk.

Recipes

No matter what method you use, salmon cooks in minutes. It is done when a small cut into the thickest part indicates that the meat flakes easily and has an even color throughout. Cooking times: 1/2 to 3/4 inch thick—cook 5–8 minutes total; 1 to 11/2 inches thick—cook 8–12 minutes total.

1. Barbecued Salmon

One salmon steak or fillet per person (cut fillets into single-serving size if necessary). Salt and pepper to taste. Rub lightly with oil (vegetable or olive). Place on grill over hot barbecue (skin side up for fillets) for 2-3 minutes. Turn over (the first side should have grill marks and be golden brown) and cook 2-3 minutes on other side, longer if the first side was light brown. After 2-3 minutes, close top of barbecue and close vents so that only small amount of air comes in, causing the fire to cool and smoke and give a smoky flavor. Add wood chips—such as hickory, oak, madrone, or alder—for flavor. Open the barbecue after 2 minutes and check by sticking fork into meat. It should flake and be opaque clear through. If meat is still pink and translucent, cook until opaque. Do not overcook.

2. Marinated Salmon

Four salmon steaks or fillets cut in serving sizes. Crush 3-4 cloves garlic with an equal amount of fresh ginger and mix with 1/2 cup soy sauce, 1 tablespoon olive oil, and 1/2 cup red or white wine. Marinate salmon for at least 1 hour or overnight in refrigerator. Marinated salmon can be barbecued (Recipe #1), broiled (#3), fried (#4), or sautéed (#5).

3. Broiled Lemon Salmon

One salmon steak or fillet cut to serving size per person. Marinate salmon (Recipe #2) or squeeze juice of half a lemon per serving into a bowl and mix with 1/2 cup olive oil per lemon. Dip each piece of salmon into juice on both sides. Place on foil under broiler on high heat. Broil until top is brown, then turn and broil other side until brown. Add 1/2 teaspoon of juice to top along with slice of lemon. (Salmon dipped in lemon juice and oil can also be barbecued.)

4. Fried Salmon

One steak or fillet per person cut into serving size, about 1/2-inch thick. Salt and pepper and fry in hot pan coated with olive or vegetable oil. Turn as soon as side becomes golden brown and cook until other side is golden brown. Flesh should flake and be opaque.

5. Sautéed Salmon

Four steaks or fillets cut to serving size per person. Brown 1/2 cup finely chopped parsley and 2 cloves finely chopped garlic with olive oil. Add salmon and turn down heat as soon as fish starts to brown. Turn and cook on other side until done (about 10 minutes or until meat is opaque).

6. Baked Salmon

One small whole salmon or piece of larger salmon. Salt and pepper inside and out. Rub with olive oil. Place in preheated 325° oven and cook for 20 minutes per inch, measured at thickest part. Check by cutting into thickest part to see if flesh is opaque.

7. Baked, Stuffed Salmon

One whole 6- to 8-pound salmon. Cut off head and tail to fit in pan or leave on. Salt and pepper inside and out. Stuff cavity with sliced tomato, bell pepper, and onion. Lay onion, pepper, and tomato slices on top and bake in preheated 325° oven for 20 minutes per inch of thickness. Test by cutting into thickest part to see if flesh is opaque.

8. Shish-kabob

Cut salmon fillets with skin on one side into 1-inch cubes. Thread cubes on skewer, alternating with cherry tomatoes and pieces of onion and bell pepper. Cook over grill or barbecue, or under broiler until done—about 5-6 minutes.

9. Poached Salmon

One small salmon or whole fillet of larger salmon. Place on greased poaching tray and immerse in cold liquid made of 1 cup white wine, 1 diced onion, and dill. Add enough water to cover salmon. Bring liquid to boil and turn down to simmer. Cook for 10 minutes per inch of thickness. Lift out on tray and serve.

10. Stir-fried Salmon

One salmon fillet with skin on, cut into 1-inch cubes. One head of cut broccoli, blanched in boiling water for 30 seconds. Drain broccoli pieces and set aside. Heat wok and stir fry 2 cloves chopped garlic, 2 teaspoons of sliced ginger root, and salmon cubes in hot oil until fish is just cooked. Then add broccoli and stir in 1 tablespoon soy sauce. Serve with rice.

11. Salmon with Salsa

Salmon in serving sizes can be broiled (Recipe #3), fried (#4), sautéed (#5), or baked (#6). Generously ladle salsa over cooked fish.

Salsa: Sauté 2 large chopped onions and 2 large, ripe diced tomatoes in 2 tablespoons olive oil until onions are translucent. Add freshly ground pepper, salt, and juice from 1 lemon.

12. Boiled Salmon Head

One large salmon head serves two people. Cover bottom of large pot with lettuce leaves to keep fish from sticking. Place salmon head on lettuce. Add 3 inches of water, 1/2 cup red or white wine, 1 onion, 2 cloves of garlic. Bring to boil and cover tightly. Lower flame and cook for 10 minutes. Serve on large plate with large bowl for scraps, skin, fins, and bones. There is a large amount of pink meat along the back of the head and the collar, and the cheeks each have a tasty piece of white meat. The more adventurous can enjoy the eyes, tongue, and meat inside the jaws. (I also enjoy much of the cartilaginous and gelatinous material in the head.) After the head is picked as clean as you desire, consume the broth.

13. Salmon Soup

One salmon carcass after it is filleted: head, backbone, fins and tail. Add onion, 2 cloves garlic, and 1 bay leaf. Boil in large pot with 1 cup white wine and 3 quarts water for about 1 hour to create 2 quarts stock. Remove head, fins, and bones, and strain liquid. Bring stock to simmer. Add 2 diced potatoes and 2 cans of juice from minced clams. Add four serving-sized pieces of salmon fillet and minced clam meat. Simmer for 10 minutes and serve in large bowls with 1 piece of salmon per serving.

Photo 6-13: Cleaned salmon.

14. Salmon Salad

Two cups of leftover cooked salmon, flaked. In large salad bowl, mix 1 clove crushed garlic, 1/2 cup olive oil, and juice of 1 lemon. Add 2 large, ripe diced tomatoes, 1 peeled, sliced cucumber, and 1 head of shredded lettuce. Add salmon and toss. Serve with freshly ground pepper and salt to taste.

15. Lomi-Lomi Salmon

Rinse fillet of salted salmon for 24 hours in cold water, changing water several times. Cut into pieces 1/4 by 1/2 inch (1 cup). Into a bowl, put 2 large, ripe tomatoes diced into 1/4-inch cubes (enough for 3 cups), 1 cup sliced green onions, and 1 cup minced cilantro. Add diced salmon and stir with 2 tablespoons white vinegar. Eat as appetizer.

Wine for Salmon

Traditionally, fish is associated with white wines. Even though a good Chablis or Chardonnay goes well with salmon, red wines are also excellent. Salmon is a rich red-meat fish and can handle red wine such as Cabernet Sauvignon or Merlot. Red wines are especially good with barbecued salmon.

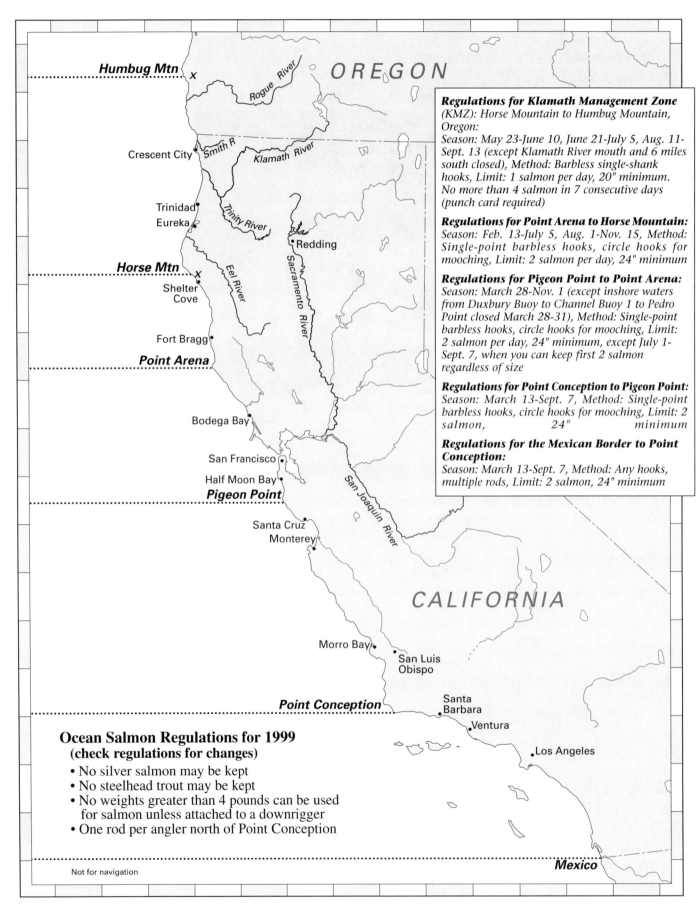

Humbug Mtn ✗

OREGON

Rogue River

Crescent City
Smith R
Klamath River

Trinidad
Eureka
Trinity River

Redding

Horse Mtn ✗
Shelter Cove
Eel River
Sacramento River

Fort Bragg

Point Arena

Bodega Bay

San Francisco

Half Moon Bay
Pigeon Point

Santa Cruz
Monterey

San Joaquin River

CALIFORNIA

Morro Bay
San Luis Obispo

Point Conception

Santa Barbara
Ventura

Los Angeles

Regulations for Klamath Management Zone
(KMZ): Horse Mountain to Humbug Mountain, Oregon:
Season: May 23-June 10, June 21-July 5, Aug. 11-Sept. 13 (except Klamath River mouth and 6 miles south closed), Method: Barbless single-shank hooks, Limit: 1 salmon per day, 20" minimum. No more than 4 salmon in 7 consecutive days (punch card required)

Regulations for Point Arena to Horse Mountain:
Season: Feb. 13-July 5, Aug. 1-Nov. 15, Method: Single-point barbless hooks, circle hooks for mooching, Limit: 2 salmon per day, 24" minimum

Regulations for Pigeon Point to Point Arena:
Season: March 28-Nov. 1 (except inshore waters from Duxbury Buoy to Channel Buoy 1 to Pedro Point closed March 28-31), Method: Single-point barbless hooks, circle hooks for mooching, Limit: 2 salmon per day, 24" minimum, except July 1-Sept. 7, when you can keep first 2 salmon regardless of size

Regulations for Point Conception to Pigeon Point:
Season: March 13-Sept. 7, Method: Single-point barbless hooks, circle hooks for mooching, Limit: 2 salmon, 24" minimum

Regulations for the Mexican Border to Point Conception:
Season: March 13-Sept. 7, Method: Any hooks, multiple rods, Limit: 2 salmon, 24" minimum

Ocean Salmon Regulations for 1999
(check regulations for changes)

- No silver salmon may be kept
- No steelhead trout may be kept
- No weights greater than 4 pounds can be used for salmon unless attached to a downrigger
- One rod per angler north of Point Conception

Not for navigation

Mexico

Map 7.1: California fishing regions and their regulations.

Chapter 7: Salmon Fishing Ports in California

Party Boat Fishing in California, 54 • Newport Beach to Point Conception, 57 • Point Conception to Pigeon Point, 59 • Pigeon Point to Point Arena, 68 • Point Arena to Horse Mountain, 84 • Horse Mountain to Humbug Mountain, 89

Photo 7-1: George Spiros with a 40-pound salmon caught trolling off the Marin County coast.

California has five ocean salmon-fishing regions plus the San Francisco Bay and Delta, as shown on Map 7.1. From south to north, the regions are
  • Newport Beach to Point Conception (Southern California),
  • Point Conception to Pigeon Point (Monterey–Santa Cruz to San Luis Obispo),
  • Pigeon Point to Point Arena (Half Moon Bay, the Gulf of the Farallones [the triangle from Point Reyes to the Farallon Islands to Pedro Point], Bodega Bay),
  • San Francisco Bay and Delta,
  • Point Arena to Horse Mountain (Fort Bragg and Shelter Cove), and
  • Horse Mountain to Humbug Mountain (Eureka, Trinidad, and Crescent City).
Map 7.1 also shows the Department of Fish and Game's regulations for each region.

Party Boat Fishing in California

My first experience with party boats was in the mid-60's. I went out of Muni Bait at Polk and Bay Streets. It had a large tackle shop and signed people up for fishing trips. It was cheap then, $10-$15. The boats left from Fisherman's Wharf. Most were heavy wooden fishing boats with benches. They had a speed of 8-10 knots, and the method was trolling, using heavy tackle and 3-pound sinkers on a release.

When I had a commercial troller berthed at the Wharf during 1970, I saw the party boats come in each day, often with limits of three fish for everyone. Most party-boat fish then, as now, were small, 20- to 25-inch salmon, weighing 5 to 9 pounds. Every once in a while the party boats would find a school of salmon over 26 inches—the minimum size for commercial salmon. These larger salmon would cause quite a stir among the commercial trollers, who would quickly get ready to make a trip and try to cash in on the bounty.

Photo 7-2: Party-boat salmon caught near the Farallon Islands.

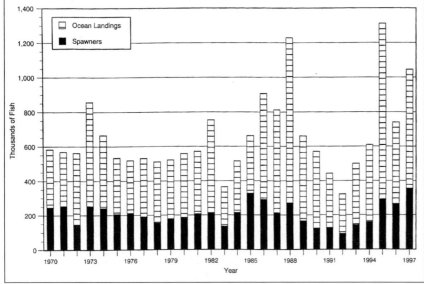

Diagram 7-1: Yearly catch and spawning record for Central California from 1970 to 1997. (Courtesy of California Department of Fish and Game.)

About 1980 many San-Francisco-Bay-Area party boat captains started converting to lighter and faster fiberglass boats, which could travel close to 20 knots and get to the fishing grounds quicker, extending their fishing range from Point Reyes in the north to south of Half Moon Bay.

Salmon fishing was hard hit during the '80s by the El Niño currents, which warmed the waters off San Francisco and closed the upwellings. There was little bait to support salmon and few salmon around. At the same time, pollution was increasing due to low water flows from the rivers. Also, more water was being shipped south, so the San Joaquin Delta pumping stations were grinding up millions of small salmon.

Salmon fishing rebounded in the waters off San Francisco in the late '80s because commercial fishing was ended and sport fishing reduced north of Fort Bragg, allowing a large number of the salmon that fed in those waters to return up the Sacramento River rather than being caught (see Diagram 7-1). Another big factor was the hatchery program, through which salmon were captured and their eggs fertilized. Millions of hatchery salmon were released. The return of the cold currents with their food-rich upwelling allowed these hatchery salmon to grow and survive. Since the late '80s salmon fishing has remained good off the coast of San Francisco.

During the early '90s, the party boats started mooching during the summer season when the salmon moved inshore to feed on the spawning anchovies. Mooching proved very popular due to the light tackle that is used.

Mooching usually starts in July around San Francisco and north, when the anchovies move into the beaches and the salmon follow and school around the bait. Half Moon Bay boats do 50/50 mooching/trolling from March through June, often because the salmon are too deep to troll. Party boats have a hard time trolling below 60 feet, so when the salmon are deep, 75-200 feet, they mooch. Monterey boats mooch year long. From Bodega Bay north, trolling is traditional.

Party-boat fishing tips

1. Pick the best time; fish when the salmon are running.
2. Research the boats, check the catch scores, and get recommendations.
3. Take seasick medication the night before (see Chapter 5).
4. Get a good night's sleep.
5. Arrive early, so you can pick your spot on the boat.
6. Dress warmly and in layers.
7. Ask the crew questions; they are there to help.
8. Use the correct tackle; call and ask beforehand.
9. Use sharp hooks.
10. Check and change your bait frequently.
11. Pay attention to your rod.
12. Duplicate the depth and bait people are using to catch fish.
13. Follow your fish around the boat; keep the fish in front of you.

Party boats off the Marin Coast

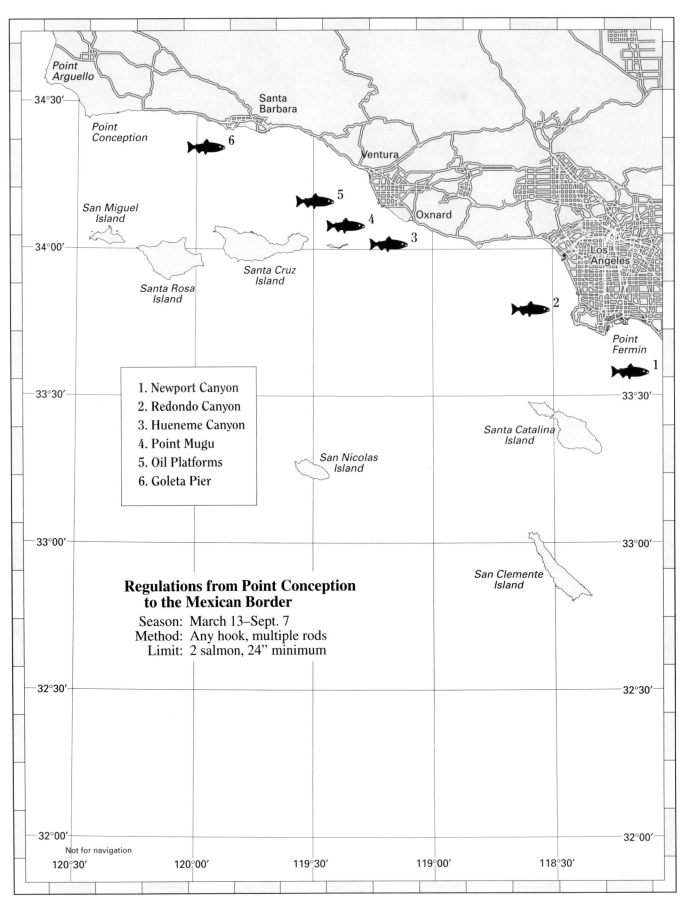

1. Newport Canyon
2. Redondo Canyon
3. Hueneme Canyon
4. Point Mugu
5. Oil Platforms
6. Goleta Pier

**Regulations from Point Conception
to the Mexican Border**
Season: March 13–Sept. 7
Method: Any hook, multiple rods
Limit: 2 salmon, 24" minimum

Map 7-2: Newport Beach to Point Conception.

Newport Beach to Point Conception: Southern California

Hot spots

Information: (310) 372-2111, (805) 985-8511, (805) 963-3564
1. Newport Canyon
2. Redondo Canyon

Photo 7-3: Santa Barbara party boat.

3. Hueneme Canyon
4. Point Mugu
5. Oil platforms
6. Goleta pier

Geography

Point Conception, known as the Cape Horn of the North Pacific, is considered the dividing line between Southern California's warm waters and Northern California's colder water (see Map 7.2). South of Point Conception, the coast runs due east for about 70 miles before it curves southeasterly along the Southern California coast. The Santa Ynez mountain range, whose western end rises from the headlands at Point Conception, closely parallels the coast and shuts off the northwest winds that blow along the outer coast and northward.

Sea and Weather Conditions

The prevailing wind is from the west and of comparatively low velocity. There are few summer storms or winds to endanger small craft. Winter storms, however, can bring heavy swells to Southern California.

Fishing

Salmon have historically followed the cold water into Southern California in the winter months to feed on the abundant schools of sardines and squid. So, even today, most years have a fair to good showing of salmon early in the season.

Salmon usually prefer the colder waters farther north, but when the water temperature is cold, about 55°, and there is a large quantity of bait fish, salmon can be found in Southern California waters. One of the best areas is off Oxnard, because of the cold upwelling from Hueneme Canyon, and most Southern-California salmon are caught between Santa Barbara and Oxnard. But salmon can show up farther south, off Newport and Redondo Canyons.

Spring is the peak time, with the best fishing from March until June. The best method is to troll at various depths until you catch a fish and then to stop and mooch. Salmon are caught deeper in Southern California, 75-200 feet, because that is where the colder water is. Often, when barracuda are found on the surface, feeding on a school of anchovies or sardines, salmon can be found feeding underneath the ball of bait. Salmon in Southern California average 16-32 pounds.

Spoons, hoochies, and anchovies are the favorite trolling baits, and threaded anchovies are preferred for mooching.

Party Boats

Most landings do not send out party boats for salmon fishing until the incidental catch starts hitting 10 to 15 salmon or they hear of a hot run. If you want to fish salmon, you need to be in contact with the landings, because some years there are only a few days of salmon fishing. For instance, in 1997, only three salmon were taken out of Oxnard, but in

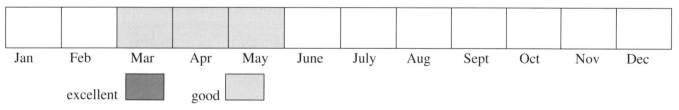

| Jan | Feb | Mar | Apr | May | June | July | Aug | Sept | Oct | Nov | Dec |

excellent ▮ good ▢

Diagram 7-2: Southern California's best salmon-fishing months.

1995 over 46,000 were landed.

Redondo Beach
Redondo Sportfishing (310) 372-2111, (310) 772-2064

Marina del Rey
Captain Frenchy's (310) 822-3625

Oxnard
Cisco's (800) 994-4852, (805) 985-8511

Santa Barbara
Sea Landing (Seahawk) (805) 963-3564

Bait and Tackle
Bait and tackle is available at the landings listed above and in Santa Monica at Lincoln-Pico Sporting Goods (310) 452-3831

Launch Facilities
Marina del Rey
Channel Islands Harbor in Oxnard
Santa Barbara

Camping
Point Mugu State Park, Oxnard, California (818) 706-1310

Photo 7-4: Marina del Rey launch ramp.

Point Conception to Pigeon Point: San Luis Obispo and Monterey-Santa Cruz

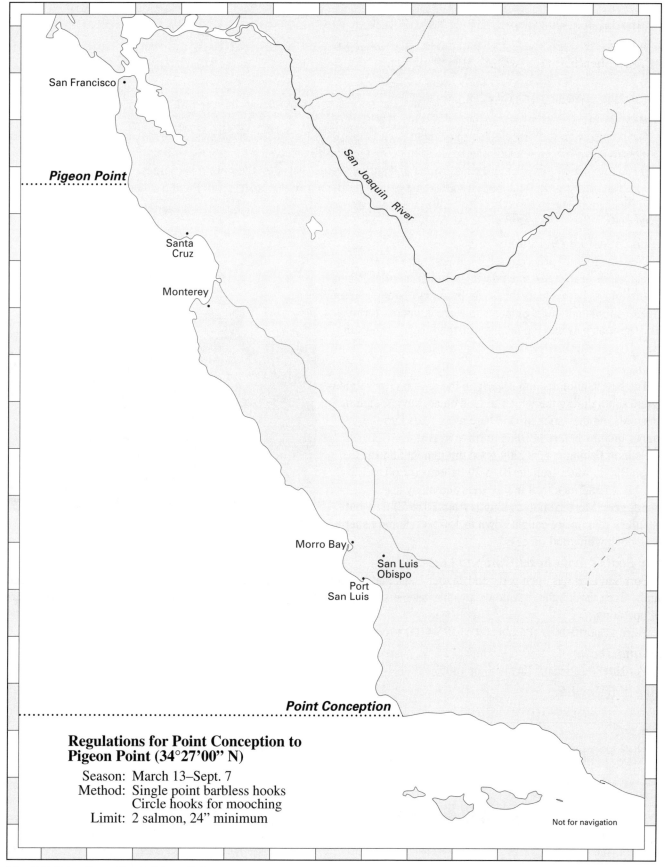

Regulations for Point Conception to Pigeon Point (34°27'00" N)

Season: March 13–Sept. 7
Method: Single point barbless hooks
Circle hooks for mooching
Limit: 2 salmon, 24" minimum

Not for navigation

Map 7-3: Point Conception to Pigeon Point

San Luis Obispo *(See map 7.4 on next page)*

Hot spots

VHF Channels 68, 14, 16

Information (805) 595-7200; Harbormaster, 805-595-5400

1. Avila Beach
2. Pismo Beach
3. Mouth of Santa Maria River

Geography

The coastline along San Luis Obispo County (see Map 7.4) is marked by broad white-sand beaches interspersed with rocky headlands. A large semicircular bay is formed by the coastline between Point Sal and Point Buchon. Salmon usually congregate in this area in the late winter and spring before they start their northward migration to begin spawning in the late summer or early fall. Often salmon are caught here into mid-summer. From Point Sal northward 20 miles to Pismo Beach, a break in the coastal hills gives way to a low coastal plain.

Sea and Weather Conditions

Prevailing winds are from the northwest, with several days of brisk winds each week, even during summer months. When the wind blows in this area, the ocean becomes choppy and too dangerous for small craft. Summer fogs are common, forming each afternoon and moving inland with the breeze as the sun sets.

Fishing

The best salmon fishing is early in the season. The salmon migrate south during the winter to feed on anchovies, sardines and squid, and they stick around here most years into the summer months before heading north to spawn.

Salmon fishing is generally good throughout San Luis Obispo Bay in water from to 10 to 20 fathoms (or 60 to 120 feet). Most fishermen troll in this area, and many use downriggers. Most salmon trolling is from 30 to 50 feet, but sometimes salmon are caught down to 150 feet. Some fishermen mooch with good success.

Photo 7-5: Vari Goddard with an 8-pound salmon.

Party Boats - Avila Beach/Port San Luis

Port San Luis has open party and charter boats that target salmon when they are running. They also have rod and reel rentals. Even though the downtown area has been disrupted by oil-company cleanup of underground spills, party boats are still operating.

Patriot Sportfishing (Patriot) (805) 595-4100 • Avila Beach Sports Fishing (Diablo) (805) 595-7200

Bait and Tackle

Portside Marine and Tackle Shop (805) 595-7214

Launching Facilities

Port San Luis pier (Avila)

Camping

Oceano Pismo State Beach (805) 489-2684 • Holiday RV Park, Pismo Beach (805) 773-1121

Oceano - Pismo Sands RV Park (800) 404-7004

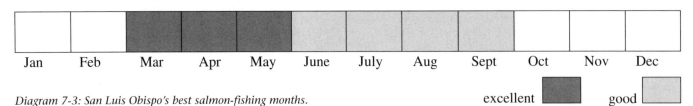

| Jan | Feb | Mar | Apr | May | June | July | Aug | Sept | Oct | Nov | Dec |

Diagram 7-3: San Luis Obispo's best salmon-fishing months.

excellent ▮   good ▯

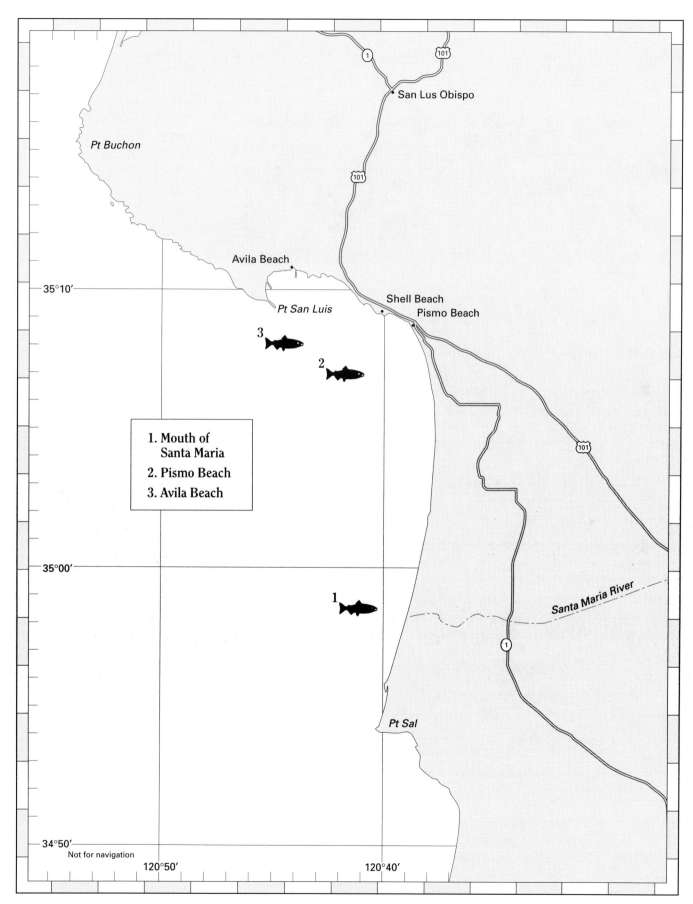

1. Mouth of Santa Maria
2. Pismo Beach
3. Avila Beach

Map 7-4: San Luis Obispo.

Morro Bay and San Simeon

Hot spots
VHF Channels 68, 14, 16
Information (805) 772-1221

Photo 7-6: Mike Berg with a salmon.

1. San Simeon
2. Cayucos
3. Toro Creek
4. Morro Rock
5. Point Buchon

Geography
From Point Estero south to Point Buchon, the coast curves in, forming Estero Bay (see Map 7.5). The hills recede, leaving a narrow coastal plain that broadens inland at Morro Bay. A sandy beach lines Estero Bay, interrupted by the towering Morro Rock that marks the entrance to Morro Bay Harbor. Morro Bay is shallow and marshy. If you don't follow its well-marked channel, you can end up stranded in the mud.

The deep water that comes in close off Point Buchon causes a strong upwelling in the Morro Bay area, creating a rich environment for bait fish and salmon, which are also attracted to the cooler water. About 30 miles northwest of Morro Bay is San Simeon, a small harbor formed by Point San Simeon.

Weather and Sea Conditions
Prevailing winds are out of the northwest. The harbor entrance is usually safe, but breakers can form and create dangerous conditions when big swells come in from offshore storms. Summer fogs are common. The coast is very rocky around San Simeon.

Fishing
Salmon fishing is very good in the Morro Bay area due to the strong upwelling of cold water. The best fishing is early in the season—March, April and May—but salmon stick around into the summer.

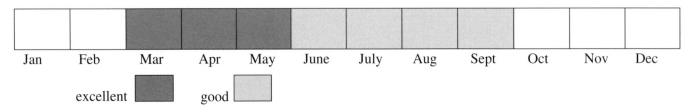

| Jan | Feb | Mar | Apr | May | June | July | Aug | Sept | Oct | Nov | Dec |

excellent ☐   good ☐

Diagram 7-4: Morro Bay–San Simeon's best salmon-fishing months.

Trolling is the method of choice here. Salmon are caught from 30 to 50 feet, but at times downriggers are used to go down to 150 feet. Some people mooch successfully, especially when a large school of salmon is concentrated on bait.

The best fishing is from Point Buchon to Cayucos in 10 to 50 fathoms (or 60 to 300 feet). Good runs sometimes develop from Morro Rock to Cayucos in 10 to 25 fathoms (or 60 to 250 feet).

Party Boats
Party boats are available out of Morro Bay whenever the salmon are running. Rods and reels can be rented, and tackle is available.

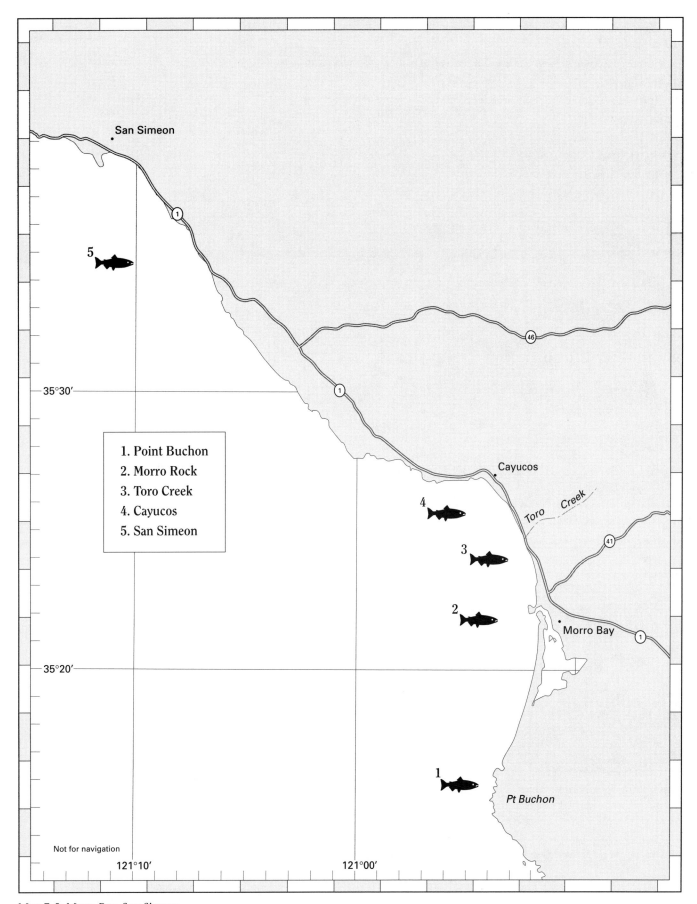

San Simeon

5

35°30'

1. Point Buchon
2. Morro Rock
3. Toro Creek
4. Cayucos
5. San Simeon

Cayucos

4

Toro Creek

3

41

2

Morro Bay

35°20'

1

Pt Buchon

Not for navigation

121°10'   121°00'

Map 7-5: Morro Bay–San Simeon.

Virg's Landing, Morro Bay (Mallard, Admiral) (805) 772-1222; (800) ROCKCOD

Bait and Tackle

Bait and tackle can be purchased at the sportfishing shops listed above.

Launch Facilities

Morro Bay

San Simeon

Camping

Morro Strand State Beach (805) 772-2560

San Simeon Creek (805) 927-2068

Bay Pine Travel Trailer Park, Morro Bay (805) 772-3223

Photo 7-7: Morro Bay fishing boats.

Photo 7-8: Morro Bay launch ramp.

Photo 7-9: Dee Dee Rodriguez with a salmon.

Monterey Bay-Santa Cruz *(See map 7.6 on next page)*

Hot spots
VHF Channels 66, 88, 11
Information (408) 475-3173, (408) 372-2203
1. Asilomar
2. Point Pinos
3. Soldiers' Club
4. Fort Ord
5. Moss Landing
6. Pajaro River
7. Sunset Beach
8. Soquel Hole
9. Cement Ship
10. Three Trees
11. Davenport

Geography
Monterey Bay is a large natural bay more than 20 miles across, stretching from Santa Cruz on the north to Monterey on the south (see Map 7.6). The Santa Cruz area is protected from the prevailing northeast wind and swells by the natural curve of the land, and Monterey is protected by Point Pinos. The harbor at Moss Landing, about halfway between Santa Cruz and Monterey, is formed by Elkhorn Slough and is protected by a jetty from Monterey north to Seacliff.

Monterey Canyon, one of the deepest sea canyons in the world, cuts through the center of Monterey Bay. Water one mile deep comes within a mile of shore at Moss Landing. This deep water creates upwellings that provide a nutrient-rich environment for all kinds of marine life.

Weather and Sea Conditions
The harbors at both Santa Cruz and Monterey are safe, with no bars to cross. Sea conditions are often light due to the protection of the bay. During the spring, however, northwest winds can make conditions dangerous. During summer, the winds are usually mild with a heavy marine layer of fog; afternoon breezes usually come up. The area off Santa Cruz is often less foggy and is sheltered from the prevailing northwest winds and swells. The area around Point Pinos and south can be rough and dangerous.

Fishing
Monterey Bay offers easy access, protected from wind and seas, to large areas of excellent salmon fishing. Small craft as well as party boats can fish this area. Monterey is where large scale mooching for salmon was introduced by the party boat fleet. Years ago, most party boats in California trolled, but in Monterey, they started mooching with a 5-ounce banana weight and an anchovy. Mooching is usually deep—from 75 to 150 or 200 feet. Trolling is also popular, but mostly with smaller private boats.

Fishing in Monterey Bay is best early in the season when the salmon congregate in the rich waters to feed on squid and sardines in the winter. As the summer progresses, the salmon start their northwest migration in preparation for spring runs up California's rivers.

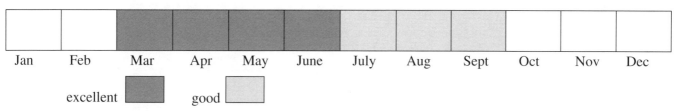

Diagram 7-5: Monterey Bay–Santa Cruz's best salmon-fishing months.

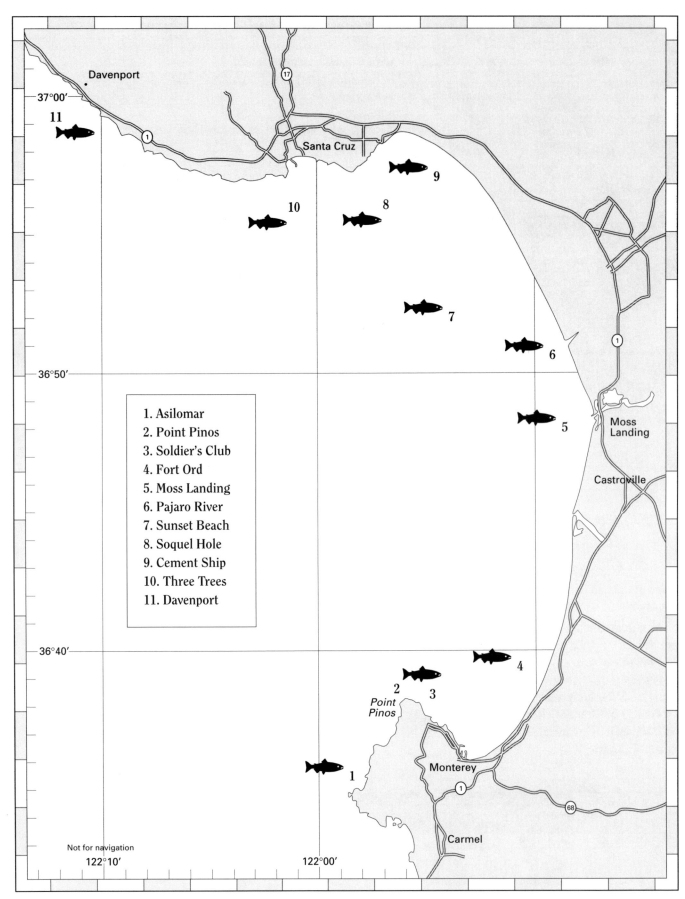

37°00′

Davenport

11

Santa Cruz

9

10

8

7

6

36°50′

1. Asilomar
2. Point Pinos
3. Soldier's Club
4. Fort Ord
5. Moss Landing
6. Pajaro River
7. Sunset Beach
8. Soquel Hole
9. Cement Ship
10. Three Trees
11. Davenport

5

Moss Landing

Castroville

36°40′

4

2

3

Point Pinos

Monterey

1

Carmel

Not for navigation

122°10′

122°00′

68

Map 7-6: Monterey–Santa Cruz.

Salmon can show up anywhere—from off of Asilomar south of Point Pinos to inside the bay off the Soldiers' Club at Fort Ord, or from Sunset Beach to Santa Cruz—in water from 60 to 250 feet deep. North of the bay, up the coast to Davenport, salmon fishing can be good, and the water is also 60- to 250-feet deep.

Party Boats

Party boats run regular salmon fishing trips out of Monterey, Moss Landing, and Santa Cruz. Most salmon fishing is mooching aboard party boats. Rods, reel and tackle can be rented.

Monterey

Monterey Sportfishing (Lethal Weapon, Magnum Force), Angelo Shake (831) 372-2203

Sam's Sportfishing (Star of Monterey, Sea Wolf) (831) 372-0577

Chris' Sportfishing (Tornado, Checkmate, Point Sur Clipper) (831) 375-5951

Randy's Sportfishing (Randy 1, Captain Randy, Sur Randy) (831) 372-7440

Santa Cruz

Bayside Tackle (831) 475-3173

Santa Cruz Sportfishing (Makaira), Judy and Ed Zoliniak (831) 426-4690

Shamrock Charters (New Holiday, Sea Dancer), Jason Young, Bill Rawson (831) 476-2648

Stagnaro's Charters (831) 423-7440

Moss Landing

Tom's Sportfishing (Kahuna), Tom and Carol Jones (831) 633-2564

Bait and Tackle

Santa Cruz Sportfishing (408) 426-4690

Bayside Marine (408) 475-2173

Breakwater Cove Deli (408) 375-6958

Fisherman's Supply (408) 476-5800

Andy's Bait and Tackle (408) 429-1925

Launch Facilities

Monterey

Moss Landing

Santa Cruz

Camping

New Brighton State Beach, Capitola (408) 475-4850

Seacliff State Beach (408) 688-3222

Sunset State Beach (408) 724-1266

Photo 7-10: Boats at the Monterey Bay wharf.

Photo 7-11: Santa Cruz party boats.

Photo 7-12: Monterey launch ramp.

Pigeon Point to Point Arena: Half Moon Bay, Gulf of the Farallones, San Francisco Bay and Delta, Bodega Bay

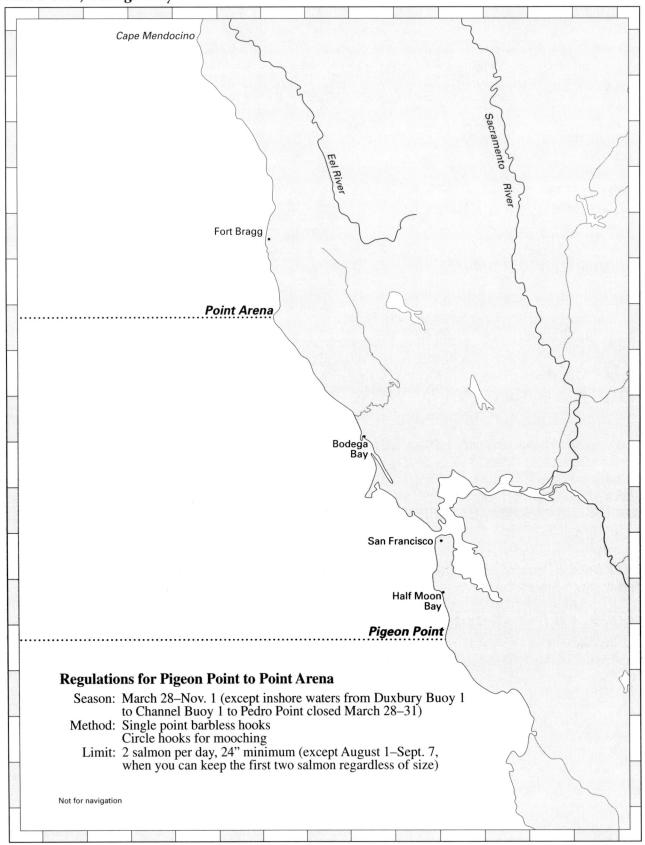

Regulations for Pigeon Point to Point Arena

Season: March 28–Nov. 1 (except inshore waters from Duxbury Buoy 1 to Channel Buoy 1 to Pedro Point closed March 28–31)

Method: Single point barbless hooks
Circle hooks for mooching

Limit: 2 salmon per day, 24" minimum (except August 1–Sept. 7, when you can keep the first two salmon regardless of size)

Not for navigation

Map 7-7: Pigeon Point to Point Arena.

Half Moon Bay

Hot spots

VHF Channels 9, 18

Information (24-hour hotline) (650) 728-0627

Photo 7-13: Mike Berg with a salmon caught off Half Moon Bay.

1. Pigeon Point
2. Martin's Beach
3. Deep Reef
4. Weather buoy
5. Miramar
6. PP (Pillar Point) Buoy
7. Egg Rock
8. Pedro Point

It was just starting to get light even though a heavy fog hung over the area. As we pulled away from the launch ramp, anchovies jumped out of the water just in front of Bart's 21-foot SeaRay as if it were a giant predator. Clearing the harbor, we put the boat on plane and, at 20 knots, we were soon out to Deep Reef. Boats were already fishing, so we put our lines in. After two hours of watching our mooching rods without a nibble while seeing other boats net small salmon, we decided to move. Either it was bad luck or we were in the wrong spot. We ran for several miles looking for greener pastures and finally stopped on a tide rip with a line of debris. We marked some bait on the fish finder and put in our lines. I had just put my rod in the holder with a threaded anchovy 25 feet down when the tip dipped slightly several times as a salmon mouthed the anchovy. I picked up the rod and felt resistance as I quickly reeled in and raised the tip high. I felt the heaviness of a nice salmon as it shook its head and then made a sizzling dash for the horizon, surfacing 50 yards away. After five minutes and several more good runs, it was alongside the boat, and Bart scooped the beautiful 12-pound salmon into the net. There was almost no breeze and it was glassy calm. At 1 p.m., we decided to head in. We had five salmon between 8 and 12 pounds among the three of us. We cleaned salmon and set them on ice in a large cooler. One short of the limit for the three of us—but a beautiful day on the ocean. As we headed back to the harbor, the fog had lifted and the hills were visible in the distance.

Geography

Half Moon Bay is a crescent-shaped bay south of Pillar Point (see Map 7.8). It is also the name of a town located about 7 miles south of Pillar Point Harbor, where the fishing boats and launch ramps are located. To further confuse things, Pillar Point Harbor is located in the town of Princeton.

Pillar Point Harbor is protected by a rock breakwater and a reef just outside. The channel is marked by buoys. Fishing is centered around Deep Reef, which is about 10 miles offshore and runs north and south for about 10 miles along the 40-fathom curve. Its rich underwater area holds bait and salmon for most of the year.

Half Moon Bay Harbor is reached by Highway 1. It is about 4 miles north of Highway 92 and about 12 miles south of Pacifica.

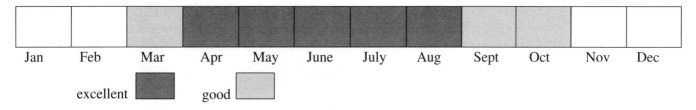

Diagram 7-6: Half Moon Bay's best salmon-fishing months.

Weather and Sea Conditions

This part of the coast attracts fog much of the time from May to September. Spring can often bring stiff northwest winds. Usual conditions are light winds and fog in the morning, with the wind coming up in the afternoon. Large swells can be dangerous when going in and out of the harbor. The reef just outside the harbor causes the large swells to build and sometimes break, especially on low tides. The channel is well marked by buoys, and it is important to follow them so you don't go over the shallow reef.

Photo 7-14: Pedro Point.

Fishing

Half Moon Bay offers easy access to good salmon fishing areas from Pedro Point on the north to Pigeon Point on the south. There is also good fishing all along Deep Reef, where most early-season fishing is centered. Salmon congregate along the rich waters to feed on krill, squid, juvenile rock cod, and anchovies. In the summer, the anchovies move into the shallow water, less than 100 feet, along the beaches to spawn. Salmon follow them, and July and August are the months to catch the largest salmon, many weighing over 20 pounds.

More and more fishermen are mooching in this area. Most of the mooching is done 20 to 40 feet down, but at times you may have to go as deep as 200 feet and use heavier weights. Trolling is also effective, especially when the salmon are not schooled up, because you can cover more water and present your bait to more fish.

Party Boats

A large party-boat fleet fishes out of Half Moon Bay. They leave daily from the docks accessible from Pillar Point pier. There is ample parking.

Captain Pete, Quite a Lady (510) 339-6848
Captain John's (650) 726-2913

Bait and Tackle

All the above sportfishing shops where you check in before boarding the boat sell bait, tackle, and licenses.

The Gear Store (650) 728-3055
Coastside #2 (415) 359-9790
Marine Warehouse (650) 728-7725

Photo 7-15: Michael Missakian with a salmon caught mooching off Pedro Point.

Launch Facilities

There is a large, modern launch for two boats at a time ($7.50 charge for launching). There are rest rooms, fish-cleaning tables with fresh water, boat wash down facilities, and a large parking lot for vehicles and trailers.

Camping

Camping is allowed overnight in the parking lot. There is also a campground about a 1/2 mile south on Highway 1.

Half Moon Bay State Beach (650) 726-8820

Photo 7-16: Tom O'Hara with a salmon caught trolling off the Marin County coast.

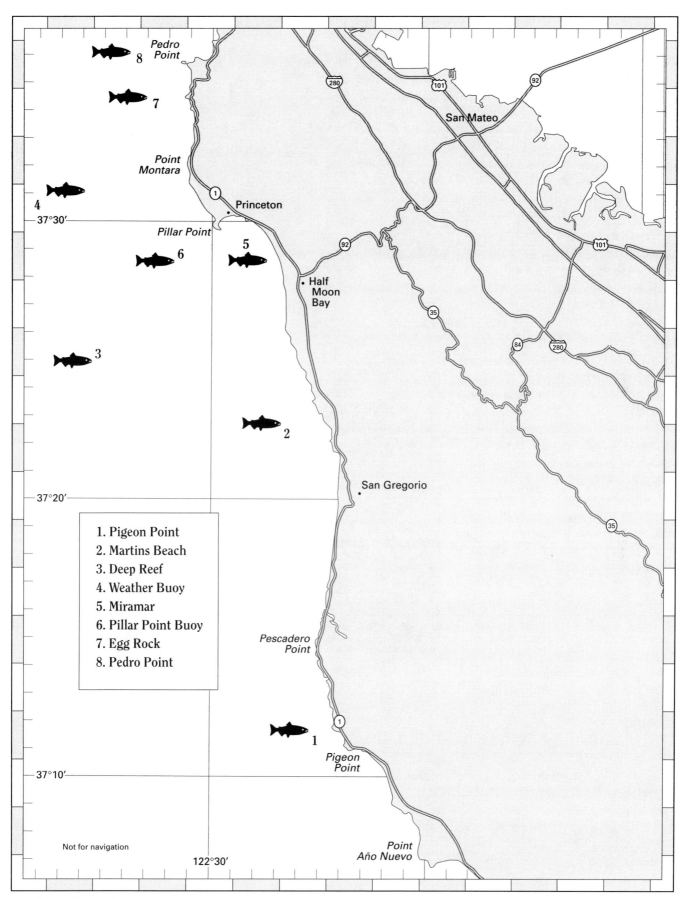

Pedro
Point
8

7

Point
Montara

4

37°30'

Pillar Point

6

5

1

Princeton

Half
Moon
Bay

3

2

San Gregorio

37°20'

San Mateo

280

101

92

92

35

84

280

101

35

1. Pigeon Point
2. Martins Beach
3. Deep Reef
4. Weather Buoy
5. Miramar
6. Pillar Point Buoy
7. Egg Rock
8. Pedro Point

Pescadero
Point

1

Pigeon
Point

37°10'

Not for navigation

122°30'

Point
Año Nuevo

Map 7-8: Half Moon Bay.

The Gulf of the Farallones: San Francisco, Emeryville and East Bay Ports, Sausalito

Hot spots

VHF Channel 67

Information (hotlines): (415) 332-1221, (510) 654-6696

1. Muir Beach
2. Rocky Point
3. Duxbury Buoy
4. Double Point
5. Point Reyes
6. Middle Grounds
7. Channel buoys
8. Lightbucket
9. S Buoy
10. W Buoy
11. N Buoy
12. Farallon Islands
13. Pedro Point

Geography

The Gulf of the Farallones is the triangle from Point Reyes on the north to the Farallon Islands (about 26 miles outside the Golden Gate) to Pedro Point off the San Mateo coast (about 15 miles south of the Golden Gate outside Point Bonita). (See Map 7.9.) The rich marine ecosystem here makes the Gulf of the Farallones one of the richest waters off the California coast. Off the Farallon Islands, the Continental Shelf falls very quickly from about 30 or 40 fathoms (or about 180 to 250 feet) down to 600 fathoms (or about 3,600 feet). The currents that hit the Continental Shelf bring up the cold, nutrient-rich water in formations called "upwellings." These upwellings rise towards the surface, bringing huge balloons of plankton and algae, which start the food chain for supporting life. As these micro-organ-

Photo 7-17: The Golden Gate Bridge shrouded in fog.

isms bloom and grow, larger organisms start feeding on them, such as krill (or small shrimp), anchovies, sardines, herring, and squid.

At the other end of the Gulf of the Farallones, San Francisco Bay, with its six-hour tidal changes, dumps huge amounts of water into the ocean. The fresh and brackish water dumped from the San Francisco Bay into the ocean creates another food-rich environment full of small organisms and sea life, supporting another food chain going the other way and adding to the richness of the Gulf of the Farallones. The tremendous tides and currents sweep food far out into the ocean, supporting many different forms of life. The effects of the tide going in and out of the Golden Gate can be felt 10 to 15 miles out to sea in the currents and the waves.

Weather and Sea Conditions

San Francisco Bay is very windy during the summer. Locals say, "The wind doesn't blow; the valley sucks." The water temperature of the Pacific Ocean off the San Francisco coast is around 50° year-round, maybe going up to 55° in the summer. The prevailing winds coming off the Pacific Ocean are cooled by the ocean waters, creating a 50° breeze. On

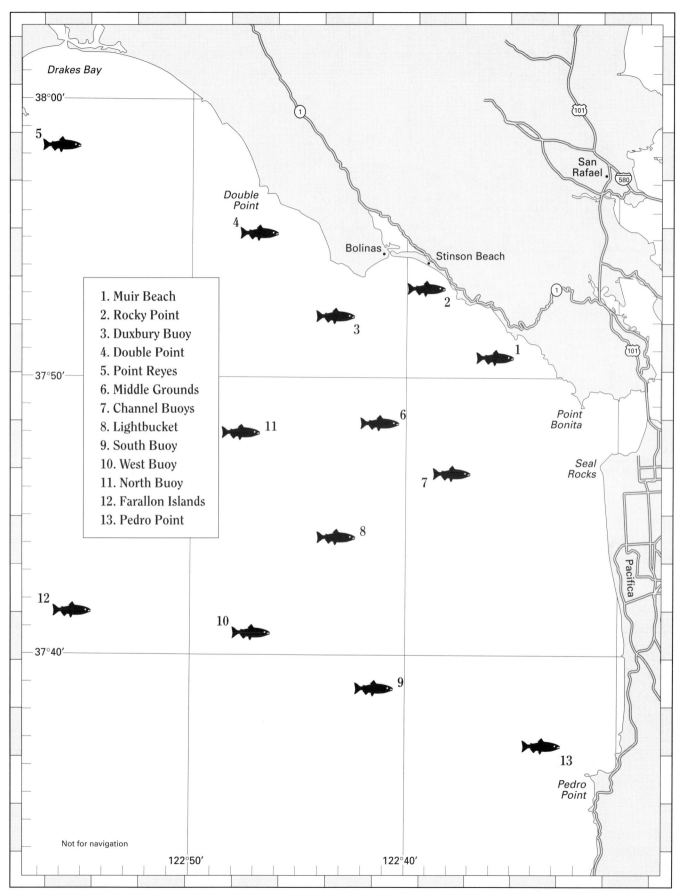

Drakes Bay

38°00′

5

Double
Point

4

Bolinas   Stinson Beach

2

3

1. Muir Beach
2. Rocky Point
3. Duxbury Buoy
4. Double Point
5. Point Reyes
6. Middle Grounds
7. Channel Buoys
8. Lightbucket
9. South Buoy
10. West Buoy
11. North Buoy
12. Farallon Islands
13. Pedro Point

37°50′

11

6

7

Point
Bonita

Seal
Rocks

8

Pacifica

12

10

37°40′

9

13

Pedro
Point

Not for navigation

122°50′   122°40′

San
Rafael

Map 7-9: The Gulf of the Farallones.

the other hand, the Central Valley of California heats up to 100° most of the summer. This hot air creates a vacuum that sucks the cold air off the Pacific in through the narrow channel at the Golden Gate. This cool air causes fog, a common summertime occurrence off San Francisco. Fog whistling in at 20 or 30 knots can cause the wind-chill factor to drop to around freezing. This is why Mark Twain said, "The coldest winter I ever spent was a summer in San Francisco."

Photo 7-18: A freighter cannot easily maneuver to avoid fishing boats.

The currents running under the Golden Gate Bridge on an outgoing tide can reach 7 knots per hour, which is as fast as some boats go. Many boats, especially sailboats, are not able to make any headway when bucking the tide against this outgoing current.

The waters outside the Golden Gate can be some of the roughest in the world, especially when the winds and storms bring in big swells off the Pacific Ocean. These swells can hit the sandbars built up by the outgoing tides north and south of the channel going out the Golden Gate. When big swells hit the sandbars, the waves increase in size and can often break, flipping over small boats and causing very rough conditions. The most famous sandbar is the "potato patch" just north of the Golden Gate, off of Point Bonita. (It is also called the "four-fathom bank," because the sandbar is 24 feet deep.) There is also a sandbar south of the channel that can be dangerous.

Navigating Precautions

The fog, wind, dangerous seas and tidal currents in the Gulf of the Farallones can all make navigating very difficult.

In 1969 I was coming down from Bodega Bay, north of Point Reyes, in "pea-soup" fog during the summer. We were navigating by compass and were lost. We finally heard waves breaking on the beach and thought we were at Point Bonita north of the Golden Gate Bridge, but it turned out we were only at Point Reyes. After we carefully headed south for many hours in the pea-soup fog, it became dark and we were lost at night in the fog somewhere in the Gulf of the Farallones. Finally, late that night, the fog cleared and we found ourselves almost out at the Farallon Islands. We had been heading south but were carried out toward the islands by an outgoing tide. Because the fog had lifted, we could see the lights of the San Francisco and the Golden Gate and we found our way in. No one should be out in the Gulf of the Farallones without some kind of electronic navigational equipment, such as GPS, Loran, or radar, in order to find their way home in the fog.

Another danger in the Gulf of the Farallones is that San Francisco Bay is a main shipping port, and freighters go in and out every day. These large freighters travel at 20 knots and take more than a mile to stop. If you are in the way, they are not able to maneuver around you. It is your duty to stay clear of freighters. In the fog, this can be difficult, because you cannot see them. If you are anywhere near the lanes where freighters are traveling and the conditions are very foggy, you must have radar to avoid being run over. Sometimes in the summer, the channel where the freighters go in and out of the bay is a hot spot for salmon, and hundreds of fishing boats congregate to fish. Whenever a freighter passes, the boats scatter to get out of the way. But if the fog is so thick that visibility is less than one hundred yards, fishing here is extremely dangerous.

One day I was fishing close to the edge of the shipping channel, and the fog came down so thick we could only see 300 or 400 yards. We could see the buoy that marks the channel. As we drifted toward the center of the channel, where the freighters usually go, I started the engine and put the boat in gear to move us back to the edge—nothing happened—we did not move. The shear pin in the propeller had broken. I panicked. Luckily, there

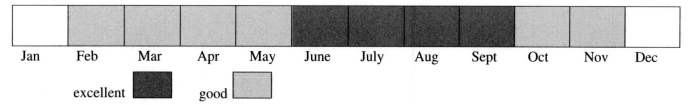

Jan	Feb	Mar	Apr	May	June	July	Aug	Sept	Oct	Nov	Dec

excellent ■   good ▨

Diagram 7-7: Gulf of the Farallones' best salmon-fishing months.

was another boat about 100 yards away. I yelled over and he agreed to tow us in. We made a line fast to the bow cleat and he started towing us. We were very relieved. Just then the fog became thicker with visibility about 100 yards, and all of a sudden we heard the loud blast of a ship's horn. We looked up, and out of the fog, less than 50 yards away, loomed a freighter going into San Francisco. If we had been 50 yards over, it would have been a tragedy.

Fishing

Most fishing in the Gulf of the Farallones is done in the area between Duxbury Buoy (about 10 miles north of Point Bonita), the Lightbucket (about 11 miles straight out from Point Bonita), and Pedro Point (about 15 miles south of Point Bonita). During the summer the salmon congregate in this area to feed on the anchovies in the inshore waters. (From Point Bonita to Duxbury Buoy, the coast of California runs just slightly north of due west, so if you go north, you head into shore; instead, your compass heading should be about 270°.)

In early spring and early summer, salmon often congregate outside this area in the deeper waters, feeding on krill and baby rock cod, near the N, W, and S buoys (for North, West and South) about 18 miles out from Point Bonita. Another 8 miles farther are the Farallon Islands.

Salmon have many favorite haunts in the Gulf of the Farallones, depending on the time of year and the food source:

1. At Duxbury Buoy, about 10 miles north of Point Bonita, deep water of about 80 feet comes up onto a 30-foot-deep reef, causing currents, upwellings, and an abundance of bait. This is a favorite spot for salmon, especially in the summer.

2. At the end of the channel buoys, deeper water, 80 to 90 feet, comes up onto the beginning of the entrance to the channel, where the water is 50 feet deep. Often bait is trapped in this area, and salmon congregate to feed on it.

3. At Pedro Point, about 15 miles to the south, again deeper water, around 80 feet, comes up onto a shallow, rocky point, with currents congregating bait.

4. At the Lightbucket, about 11 miles off Point Bonita, in the 90-foot water in the center of the Gulf of the Farallones, tides and currents often concentrate bait fish.

5. Seven miles north, west, or south of the Lightbucket are the N, W, and S buoys in water about 180 feet deep. These areas often hold salmon earlier in the year when shrimp or krill congregate.

Photo 7-19: Bart Ribotta with two salmon caught mooching off Stinson Beach.

Photo 7-20: San Francisco party boats.

6. During the summer, usually about July first, the anchovies make their spawning arrival at the beaches up and down the coast off San Francisco. The salmon follow them in and are found close to the beaches all the way from Duxbury to Pedro Point in shallow water, from 30 to 100 feet.

Party Boats

A large number of party boats are usually available. Reservations are advised on weekends, especially when the salmon are running.

San Francisco

Wacky Jacky (Jackie Douglas) (415) 587-1467, 586-9800
Butchie B (Pat Bentivegna) (415) 457-8388
New Edibob (Bob Barg) (415) 564-2706
Lovely Martha (Frank Rescino) (415) 871-1691

Emeryville

Emeryville Sportfishing Center (Craig Stone, Frank Salazar) (510) 654-6040, hotline (510) 654-6696

Sausalito

Caruso's Sportfishing (415) 332-1015, hotline (415) 332-1221
Flying Fish (Brian Guiles) (415) 898-6610
Ginnie C II (Jim Robertson) (415) 454-3191
Salty Lady (Roger Thomas) (415) 348-2107
New Rayann (John Atkinson) (415) 924-6851
Pacific Queen (Ron Nass) (415) 479-1322
New Merrimac (Taylor McGee) (415) 388-5351
Louellen (Andy Petterson) (415) 664-9619

Photo 7-21: Michael Missakian with a 10-pound salmon caught mooching off San Francisco.

Other Party Boats

Oyster Point

Jim Cox Sportfishing (415) 369-3807

Bait and Tackle

G and M Sales, San Francisco (415) 863-2855
Hi's Tackle Box, San Francisco (415) 221-3825
Jailhouse Bait and Tackle, Brisbane (415) 468-7887
Western Boat Shop, San Rafael (415) 456-5454
Loch Lomond Bait and Tackle, Loch Lomond (San Rafael) (415) 456-0321
Siegle's, Oakland (510) 655-8789

Launch Facilities

Sausalito

Caruso's. Take Highway 101 and turn off at Sausalito. Take Bridgeway to Harbor Drive and follow toward the Bay.

San Francisco

Mission Rock—but the pier has been in poor shape in recent years. Take Highway 280 to the Mariposa exit; follow Mariposa to the Bay and turn left on China Basin; go about 1 mile.

Berkeley—good ramp. Take Highway 80 to University Avenue exit and follow University toward the Bay; turn right on Marina to reach launch ramp.

Oakland—good ramp, free. Take Highway 880 to 18th Street exit; turn left on Embarcadero and go about 1 mil to reach the launch ramp.

Alameda (off Clement)—good ramp and pier, free. Take Highway 880 to 22nd Street exit; go over Park Street Bridge to Buena Vista Avenue; turn right and go about 1 mile to Grand; turn right to reach launch ramp.

Oyster Point—good launch. Take Highway 101 to Oyster Point Boulevard, which is just south of San Francisco; follow Oyster Point Boulevard to Oyster Point Marina and the launch ramp.

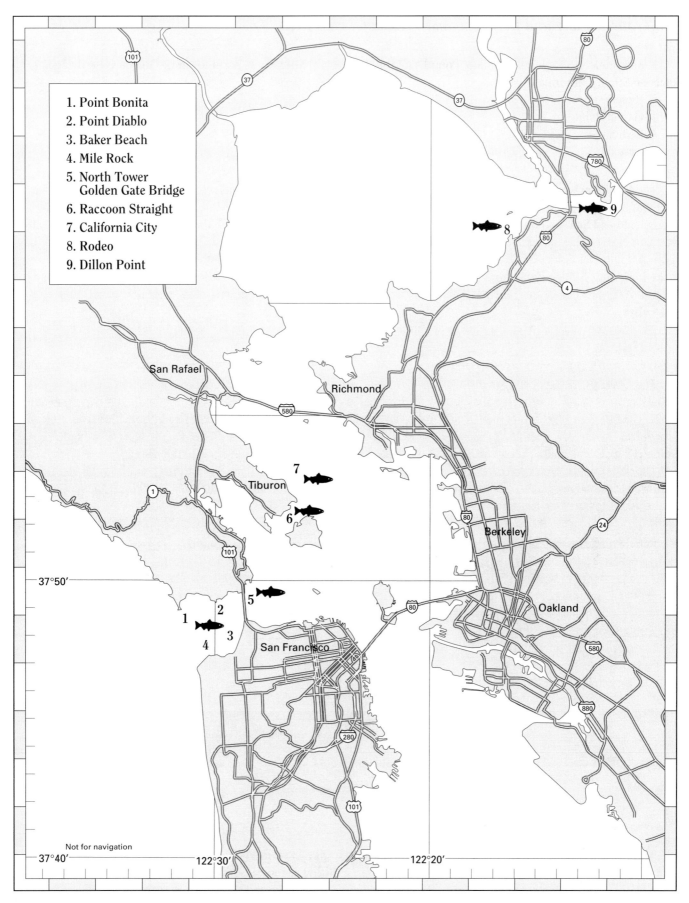

1. Point Bonita
2. Point Diablo
3. Baker Beach
4. Mile Rock
5. North Tower
   Golden Gate Bridge
6. Raccoon Straight
7. California City
8. Rodeo
9. Dillon Point

Map 7-10: San Francisco Bay and Delta.

San Francisco Bay and Delta *(See map 7.10 on previous page)*

Hot spots

1. San Francisco Bay: Point Bonita, Point Diablo, Baker Beach, Mile Rock, north tower of Golden Gate Bridge, Raccoon Strait, California City
2. Rodeo
3. Garnet Point
4. Benicia
5. Antioch

Geography

The San Francisco Bay is a large body of water (60 miles long by 15 miles at its widest) that drains the Santa Clara Valley to the south and the Petaluma and Napa Rivers to the north (see Map 7.10). Most of its water comes from the Sacramento and San Joaquin Rivers and their tributaries, which enter the bay through the Carquinez Straits in the north-west corner of the bay. Much of the bayshore has been filled, so the bay is significantly smaller than it was once. The bay is divided into San Francisco Bay, from Point Richmond south to San Jose, and San Pablo Bay, from Point Richmond east to the Carquinez Straits. From the Carquinez Straits to Pittsburg is Suisun Bay. Above Pittsburg where the Sacramento and San Joaquin Rivers come together is the beginning of the Delta with its thousands of miles of interconnecting waterways.

All this water exits into the Pacific Ocean through a narrow, one-mile opening in the coastal hills spanned by the Golden Gate Bridge.

Weather and Sea Conditions

The Golden Gate Bridge separates two very different climates. Outside is the Pacific Ocean's cold (low 50s) up-welling created by the northwest winds. Inside the bridge, the climate is protected by the coastal hills running north and south. The interior of California (the Central Valley and Delta) has a very warm climate, often hitting 100° from June to September. This hot air rises and creates low pressure that sucks the cold, moist air off the Pacific Ocean through the Golden Gate, often creating fog with 20+ knot winds in the bay, especially on summer afternoons.

The bay from the Golden Gate to the Carquinez Straits can be dangerous when these winds combine with large tides to create short, choppy waves. Currents can sometimes reach 7 knots under the Golden Gate. Small boats can get in trouble here, and ones under 16 feet can be dangerous.

Fishing

Salmon typically enter the bay on their way up to their spawning grounds in the summer. They seem to congregate in an area called "California City," where the water is over 100 feet deep. You won't find California City on the map; it is the water just north of Raccoon Straits between Bluff Point and Chauncey Point that separates the Tiburon Peninsula from Angel Island. Salmon hold in the deep water behind Tiburon, especially in the late summer and early fall. They seem to stay only for a couple of days before heading up river. So you have to be there on the right day. High tide and the two hours afterward is the best time.

Another spot for salmon fishing is the waters from the north tower of the Golden Gate Bridge up to Raccoon Straits. This area is sometimes good in the summer when large concentration of anchovies enter the bay. It is best on the incoming tide, especially at the top of the tide.

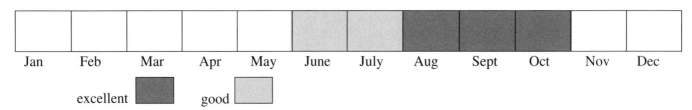

Diagram 7-8: San Francisco Bay and Delta's best salmon-fishing months.

Trolling is the method of choice inside the bay, because the salmon seem to be more dispersed and trolling is better than mooching to cover a lot of water. Salmon will also take a drifted anchovy, but you need a lot of patience.

Although less common, there are times when salmon hold off the north and south towers of the Golden Gate Bridge and off the San Francisco Marina. Sometimes there will be salmon off the west end of the Bay Bridge, and at times off the west end of Treasure Island.

Bay fishing for salmon is a matter of timing. You must be there when the salmon are in, because they don't stay long. However, salmon are caught incidentally throughout the year inside the bay, mostly while people are fishing for stripers and halibut.

Party Boats

Because salmon are not very predictable inside the bay and delta, party boats do not specifically target them. Salmon party boats that fish in the ocean will come into the bay to fish salmon when a good run develops or the salmon disappear from the ocean, or when the weather is so bad on the ocean that they have no other choice. (For names and numbers of party boats, see Gulf of Farallones section.)

Bait and Tackle

G and M Sales, San Francisco (415) 863-2855

Hi's Tackle Box, San Francisco (415) 221-3825

Jailhouse Bait and Tackle, Brisbane (415) 468-7887

Western Boat Shop, San Rafael (415) 456-5454

Loch Lomond Bait and Tackle, Loch Lomond (San Rafael) (415) 456-0321

Siegle's, Oakland (510) 655-8789

Launch Facilities

Sausalito

Caruso's. Take Highway 101 and turn off at Sausalito. Take Bridgeway to Harbor Drive and follow toward the Bay.

San Francisco

Mission Rock—but the pier has been in poor shape in recent years. Take Highway 280 to the Mariposa exit; follow Mariposa to the Bay and turn left on China Basin; go about 1 mile.

Berkeley—good ramp. Take Highway 80 to University Avenue exit and follow University toward the Bay; turn right on Marina to reach launch ramp.

Oakland—good ramp, free. Take Highway 880 to 18th Street exit; turn left on Embarcadero and go about 1 mil to reach the launch ramp.

Alameda (off Clement)—good ramp and pier, free. Take Highway 880 to 22nd Street exit; go over Park Street Bridge to Buena Vista Avenue; turn right and go about 1 mile to Grand; turn right to reach launch ramp.

Oyster Point—good launch. Take Highway 101 to Oyster Point Boulevard, which is just south of San Francisco; follow Oyster Point Boulevard to Oyster Point Marina and the launch ramp.

Shore Fishing in the San Francisco Bay and Delta

San Francisco Bay and Delta (see Map 7.10) offer the opportunity for the angler without a boat to catch salmon from shore. The pier at Pacifica, 15 miles south of San Francisco, offers salmon angling in the ocean. In San Francisco, the public piers at Fort Point and Fort Mason offer salmon fishing from shore, which is best in the late summer and early fall when the salmon enter the bay on their way upstream to spawn. On the Marin County side of the Golden Gate Bridge, you can fish from the pier at Fort Baker.

The technique is to rig a dead anchovy under a baseball-sized orange styrofoam float and wait until a salmon comes along and eats the bait. You will also need a crab net to lower under the played-out salmon and hoist it onto the pier.

Fort Point Pier

To get there, follow the signs to Crissy Field from Marina Boulevard. Continue west to the last parking lot, where the pier is located.

Fort Mason Pier

The entrance to Fort Mason is at the intersection of Buchanan Street and Marina Boulevard. Turn right into Fort Mason's gates opposite the Marina Safeway; a parking lot is on the other side of the entrance.

Fort Baker

Take the Alexander Avenue exit off Highway 101 just north of the Golden Gate Bridge. The turn off is to the right. Follow the signs to Fort Baker.

Rodeo

Shoreline fishing for salmon is available at Rodeo, where salmon pass close to the shore off the railroad tracks as they make their way upstream to spawn. Most anglers cast either spinners or spoons. Rodeo is reached by taking the Rodeo exit off Highway 80 and proceeding west until you reach the bay.

Dillon Point

Just north of the Carquinez Bridge is Dillon Point, where salmon also pass close to shore. Casting spinners and spoons is the method used here. To get to Dillon Point, take Highway 780 east to the first exit and follow it down to Glen Cove. Park along the water.

Pittsburg

Farther up river at the town of Pittsburg there is a rock-wall jetty just below the harbor that salmon pass. Casting spinners and spoons is the most popular method of catching salmon. To get to Pittsburg, take the Railroad Avenue exit off Highway 4 until you reach the harbor. Then proceed to the end of the rock wall at the west end of the harbor.

Photo 7-21a Miguelina Perez with Fort Baker and Fort Point in background.

Bodega Bay *(See map 7.11 on next page)*

Hot spots

VHF Channels 68, 77, 88
Information (707) 875-2323

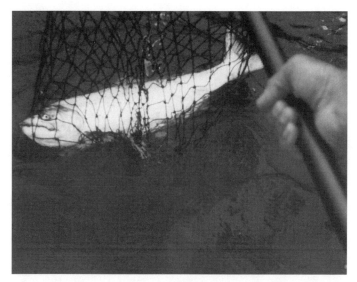

Photo 7-23: A netted 20-pound salmon caught off Bodega Bay.

Photo 7-22: Bodega Bay harbor is home to a large commercial fishing fleet. (Photo courtesy of Tom O'Hara.)

1. Point Reyes
2. Elephant Rock
3. Tomales Point
4. Whistle Buoy
5. Salmon Creek
6. Carmet
7. Fort Ross

Geography

Bodega Bay is a naturally protected bay that lies off Highway 1 between Tomales Bay and Jenner (see Map 7.11). The ocean drops off to 10 fathoms within a mile of the harbor and often you can catch salmon there. One of the attractions for small boaters is the close-in fishing for large salmon. Fishing can be good anywhere along the coast from Point Reyes in the south to Fort Ross in the north. However, the best areas are off Tomales Point, about 5 miles south of the harbor, and Elephant Rock, which is just south of Tomales Point. In the north, the best areas are Salmon Creek, about 4 miles, and Carmet, about 2 miles farther north.

Weather and Sea Condition

This part of the coast is often foggy during June, July, and August. Visibility can be less than 1/4 mile at times, so good compass navigation or a GPS or radar is necessary. During the spring, winds out of the northwest blow for days on end, making it difficult to fish. Bodega Head protects the entrance to the harbor from the prevailing northwest swell. Like most of Northern California, winds are usually light in the mornings, and the northwest wind comes up in the afternoon.

Fishing

Bodega Bay offers easy access to good salmon fishing starting within one mile of the harbor. Trolling is the most popular method here, but more boats are starting to use mooching techniques.

Party Boats

Party boats are available out of Bodega, but because rock cod fishing is so popular here, sometimes only one boat is available for salmon.

The Boathouse, 1445 Highway 1, Bodega Bay 94923 (707) 875-3344

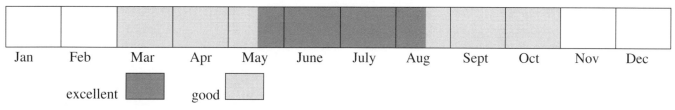

Diagram 7-8: Bodega Bays best salmon-fishing months.

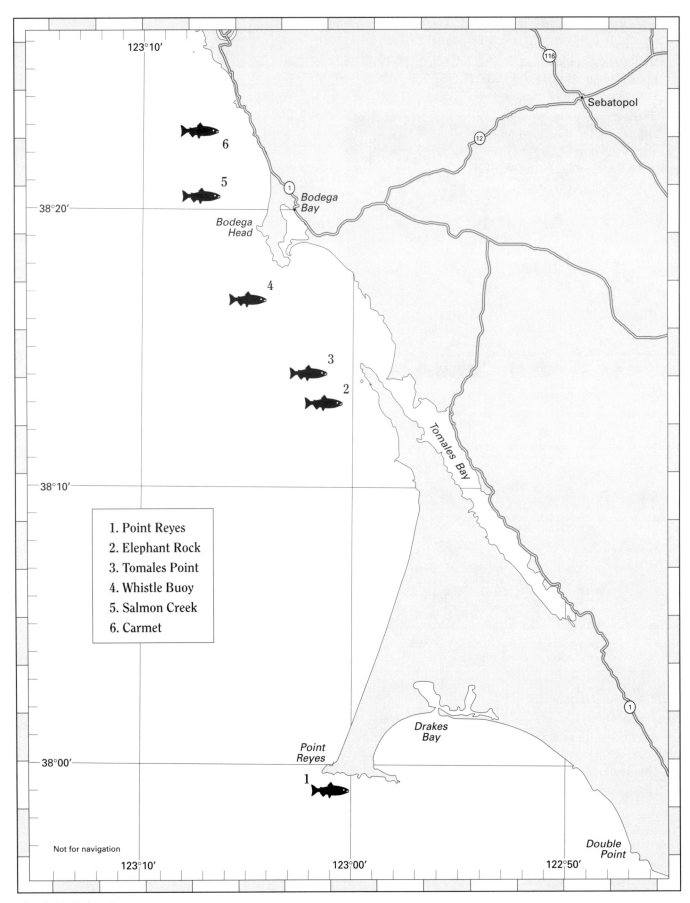

1. Point Reyes
2. Elephant Rock
3. Tomales Point
4. Whistle Buoy
5. Salmon Creek
6. Carmet

Map 7-11: Bodega Bay.

Wil's Fishing Adventures (Tracer, Payback) (707) 875-2323
New Sea Angler, Bodega (707) 875-3495
Bodega Bay Sportfishing Center, 1500 Bay Flat Road (Predator, Jaws), Rick Powers (707) 875-3344
Porto Bodega, Bodega Bay (707) 875-3495
Jaws Sportfishing, Bodega Bay (707) 875-3495

Bait and Tackle
The Boathouse (707) 875-3344
Porto Bodega (707) 875-3495
Wil's Fishing Adventures (707) 875-2323
Outdoor Pro Shop, Rohnert Park (707) 588-8033

Launch Facilities
Doran Park (707) 875-3540
Shaw's Marina
Westside Park

Camping
There is camping at both Doran Park, (707) 875-3540, and Westside Park.
Bodega Dunes, Sonoma State Beach (707) 895-3483

Photo 7-24: Mike Berg with a salmon caught while mooching.

Point Arena to Horse Mountain: Fort Bragg and Shelter Cove

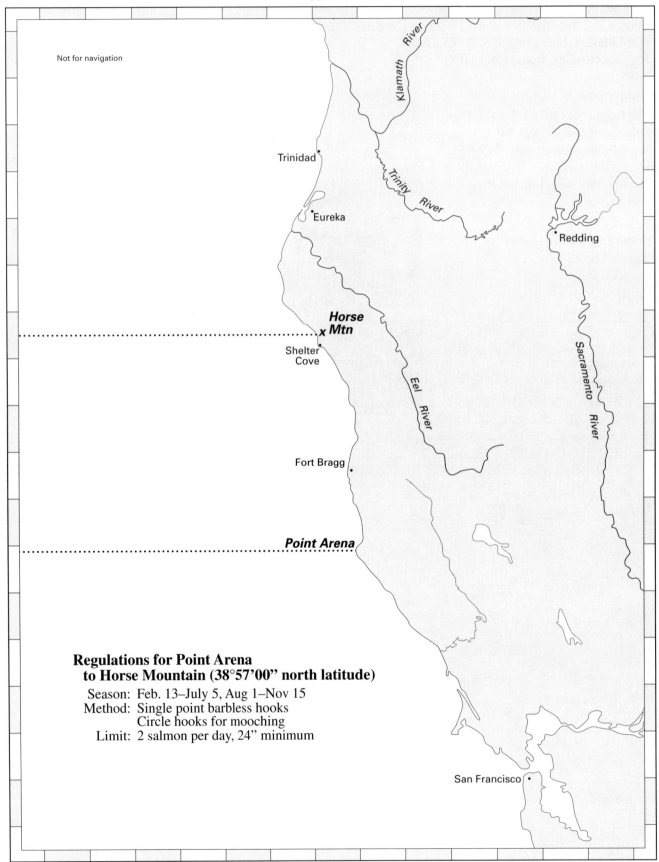

Not for navigation

Klamath River

Trinity River

Trinidad

Eureka

Redding

Horse x Mtn

Shelter Cove

Eel River

Sacramento River

Fort Bragg

Point Arena

**Regulations for Point Arena
to Horse Mountain (38°57'00" north latitude)**
Season: Feb. 13–July 5, Aug 1–Nov 15
Method: Single point barbless hooks
Circle hooks for mooching
Limit: 2 salmon per day, 24" minimum

San Francisco

Map 7-12: Point Arena to Horse Mountain.

Fort Bragg *(See map 7.13 on next page)*

Hot spots

Information (707) 964-4550
1. Little River
2. Point Cabrillo
3. Casper Point
4. Hard Creek
5. Whistle buoy
6. MacKerricher State Park

Geography

Noyo Harbor is formed by the Noyo River emptying into a small, natural indentation in the coast (see Map 7.13). It is on Highway 1, about a mile north of the intersection with Highway 20.

Weather and Sea Conditions

As in most of Northern California, fog abounds most of the summer. Spring winds can kick up northwest swells that make it hard for boats to get out. Check wind and sea conditions before going out and have good navigational equipment in case you have to find your way in the fog.

Photo 7-25: Alfred Kuo admiring a nice salmon caught while mooching.

Fishing

Sportfishing boats operate out of Noyo Harbor, and trolling is the most popular method. The area in front of the harbor and several miles in either direction is where you find the salmon. Fish the water from 10 to 60 fathoms (or 60 to 360 feet). Most small boats fish within 3 miles of the whistle buoy, located about a mile west of the mouth of the Noyo River. Salmon fishing usually starts later here, in May, and peaks in June and July.

Party Boats

Anchor Charter Boats (707) 964-4550   Lady Irma, Fort Bragg (707) 964-3854
Tallyho II, Fort Bragg (707) 964-2079   Misty II, Fort Bragg (800) 475-4514
Telstar Charters, Randy Thornton (707) 964-8770

Bait and Tackle

Patty-C Charter Fishing, Noyo Harbor (707) 964-0669   Noyo Fishing Center, Fort Bragg (707) 964-7609
Fireo's Chevron Station (707) 964-5174

Launch Facilities

Noyo Harbor

Camping

MacKerricher State Park, about 3 miles north on Highway 1 (707) 937-5804
Van Damme State Park, about 14 miles south on Highway 1 (707) 937-5804
Russian Gulch State Park, about 10 miles south on Highway 1 (707) 937-5804

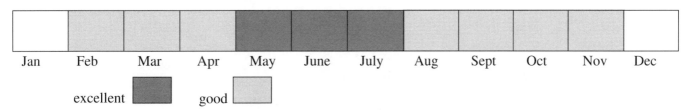

Diagram 7-10: Fort Bragg's best salmon-fishing months.

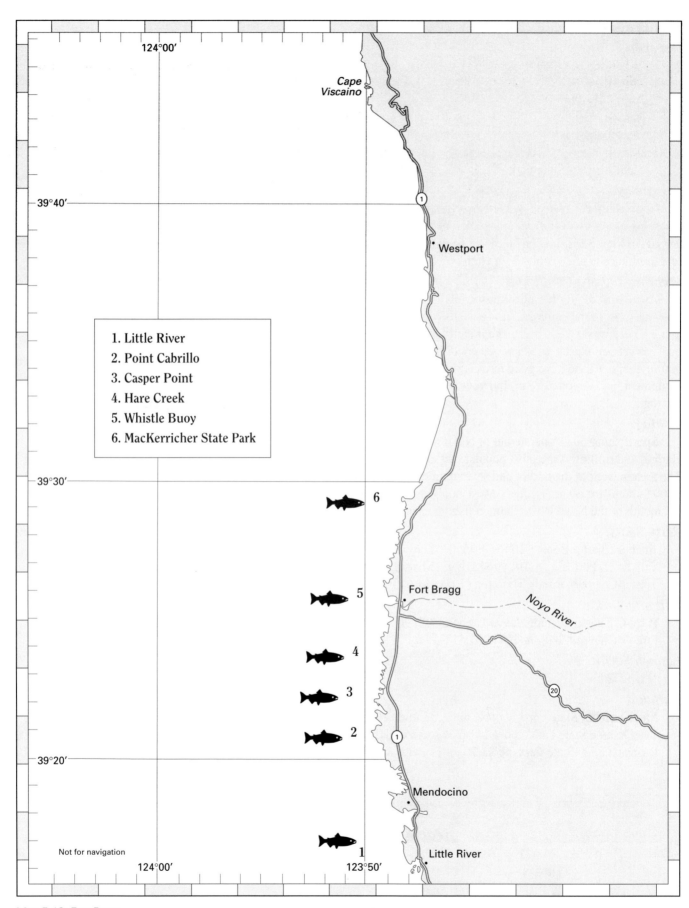

1. Little River
2. Point Cabrillo
3. Casper Point
4. Hare Creek
5. Whistle Buoy
6. MacKerricher State Park

Map 7-13: Fort Bragg.

Shelter Cove (See map 7.14 on next page)

Hot spots

    CB Channel 15

    Information (707) 986-7624

    1. Tolo Bank

    2. Whistle Buoy

    3. Point Delgada

    4. Dead Man's Beach

Geography

    Shelter Cove is reached by taking Briceland Road off Highway 101 at Garberville for about 25 miles through the isolated coastal hills. The road is good, but it has some windy and steep parts. Shelter Cove is formed by Point Delgada, which protects it from the prevailing northwest winds and swells (see Map 7.14). Delgada Canyon is a deep underwater canyon that comes in just north of Point Delgada and provides a nutrient-rich upwelling, making the area very productive for salmon as well as many other fish.

Photo 7-26: Alfred Kuo with a salmon caught mooching an anchovy.

    Lost Coast Sportfishing (707) 986-7624

Launch Facilities

    Launching is available by driving down on the flat, hard-packed, sandy beach and backing your trailer into the protected water of Shelter Cove.

Camping

    Shelter Cove Campground (707) 986-7474

Weather and Sea Conditions

    Because Point Delgada usually protects the cove and there is launching from the beach, it is an ideal place for small boats. However, when winds or swells come from the west or south, the cove is unprotected and can be unfishable for small boats. As in much of Northern California, fog abounds during the summer months, and navigational aids are necessary, at least a compass.

Fishing

    Shelter Cove provides great salmon fishing, especially during June, July, and August, when large schools of king salmon feed in the fertile waters offshore. Most people troll in this area, but mooching also works and is becoming popular. Most of the fishing takes place within a couple of miles of the Bell and Whistle Buoys.

Party Boats

    Party boats and boat rentals are available at Mario's Marina, Bud Lair (707) 986-7432

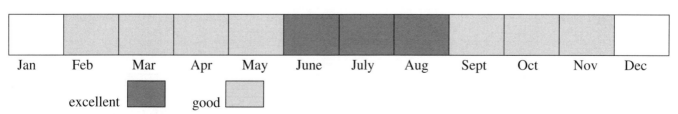

Diagram 7-11: Shelter Cove's best salmon-fishing months

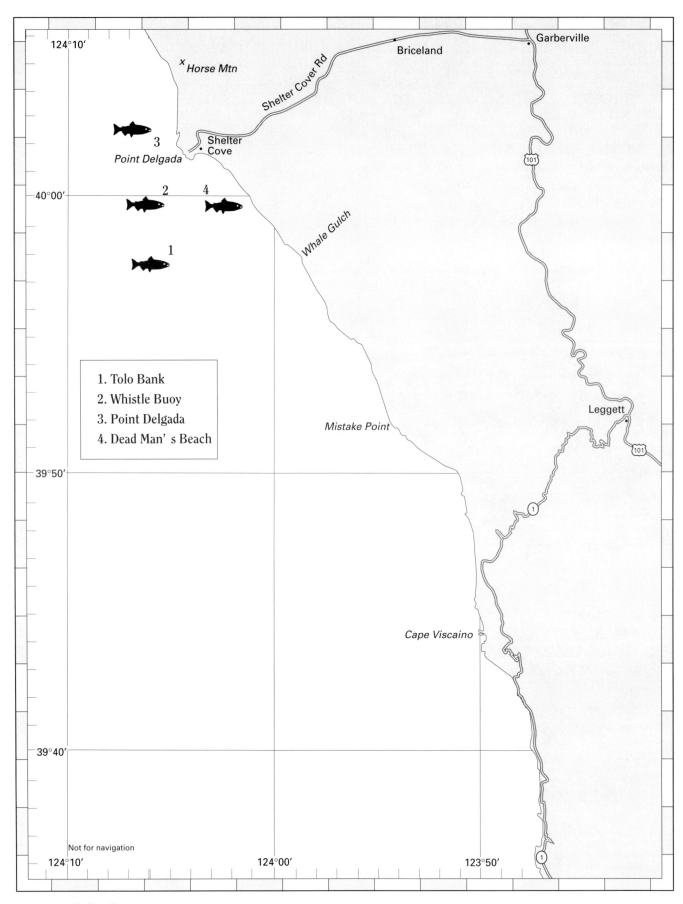

Map 7-14: Shelter Cove.

Horse Mountain to Humbug Mountain: Eureka, Trinidad, and Crescent City

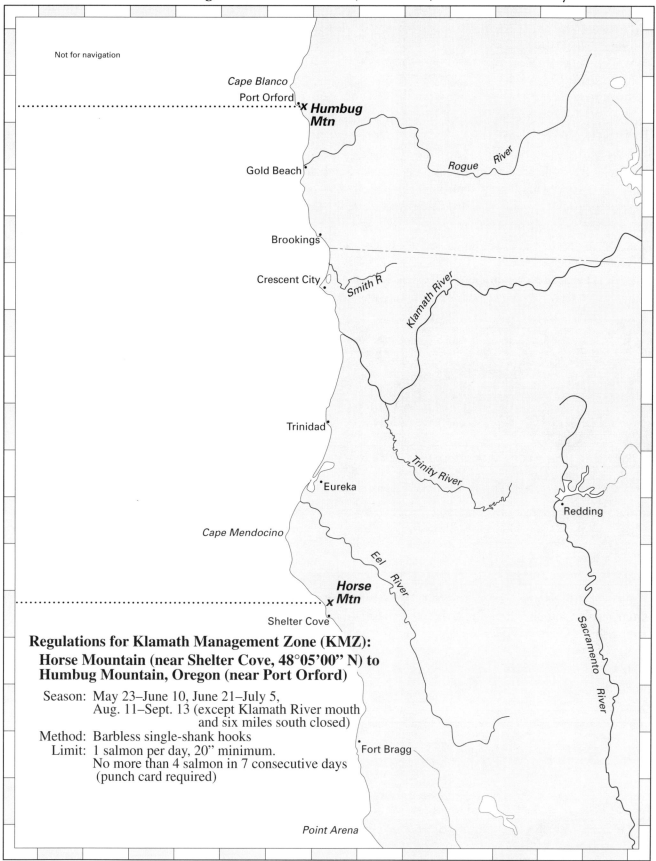

Not for navigation

Cape Blanco
Port Orford **x Humbug Mtn**

Rogue River

Gold Beach

Brookings

Crescent City

Smith R

Klamath River

Trinidad

Trinity River

Eureka

Redding

Cape Mendocino

Eel River

Horse x Mtn

Shelter Cove

Regulations for Klamath Management Zone (KMZ):
Horse Mountain (near Shelter Cove, 48°05'00" N) to Humbug Mountain, Oregon (near Port Orford)

Season: May 23–June 10, June 21–July 5,
   Aug. 11–Sept. 13 (except Klamath River mouth
      and six miles south closed)
Method: Barbless single-shank hooks
 Limit: 1 salmon per day, 20" minimum.
   No more than 4 salmon in 7 consecutive days
    (punch card required)

Fort Bragg

Sacramento River

Point Arena

Map 7-15: Horse Mountain to Humbug Mountain.

Eureka-Humboldt Bay *(See map 7.16)*

Hot spots

CB Channel 11
Information (707) 442-3474

1. Whistle buoy
2. North Jetty
3. South Jetty
4. Mouth of Eel River
5. Mouth of Mad River

Geography

Humboldt Bay is the major port in California north of San Francisco (see Map 7.16). The natural bay extends for more than 20 miles in a north-south direction. It empties into the ocean through a relatively narrow mouth, about one mile wide. Because this is a major lumber and fishing port, there is considerable shipping traffic in and out of the harbor.

Weather and Sea Conditions

This part of the coast can have rough seas and heavy winds. Close attention to wind and sea conditions is a must before venturing outside the bay.

The bar is located on the north jetty and extends into the ocean for at least half a mile. It is dangerous, especially during rough weather, but even in calm weather, outgoing tides can cause steep, dangerous breakers. Call the Coast Guard for up-to-date conditions before deciding to go out: (707) 433-7062 (recording) or (707) 443-2212.

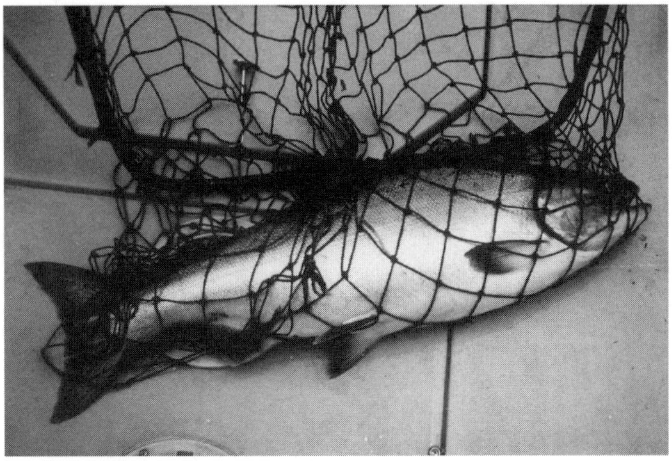

Photo 7-27: A salmon from Trinidad in the net.

Fishing

During the summer months, salmon move into the beaches and around the jetties at the harbor entrance. On calm days, small boats can make it out into the ocean and fish the areas surrounding the harbor entrance. Most fishing is in the vicinity of the Whistle Buoy.

Trolling is the most popular method, and many people use downriggers. Bait, either anchovies or herring, is the most popular way to troll. Lures, such as a plastic squid (or hoochie) rigged 18 inches behind a flasher, are also widely used. Mooching is becoming more common, especially when large schools of salmon drive masses of anchovies into the harbor entrance.

Party Boats

Party boats fish salmon when in season and the weather cooperates.
Grundman's Sporting Goods. Rio Dell, (707) 764-5744
King Salmon Charters (707) 442-3474
Celtic Charters (707) 442-2580

Launch Facilities

Fields Landing
King Salmon
Samoa (can have rapid cross-currents at peak tides)

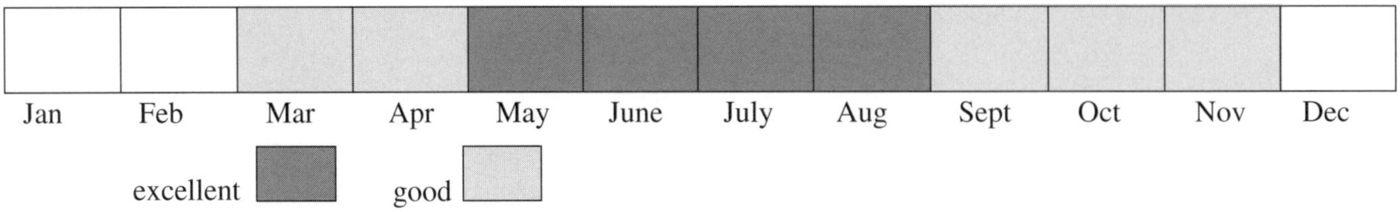
Jan
Feb
Mar
Apr
May
June
July
Aug
Sept
Oct
Nov
Dec
excellent
good

Diagram 7-12: Eureka–Humboldt Bay's best salmon-fishing months.

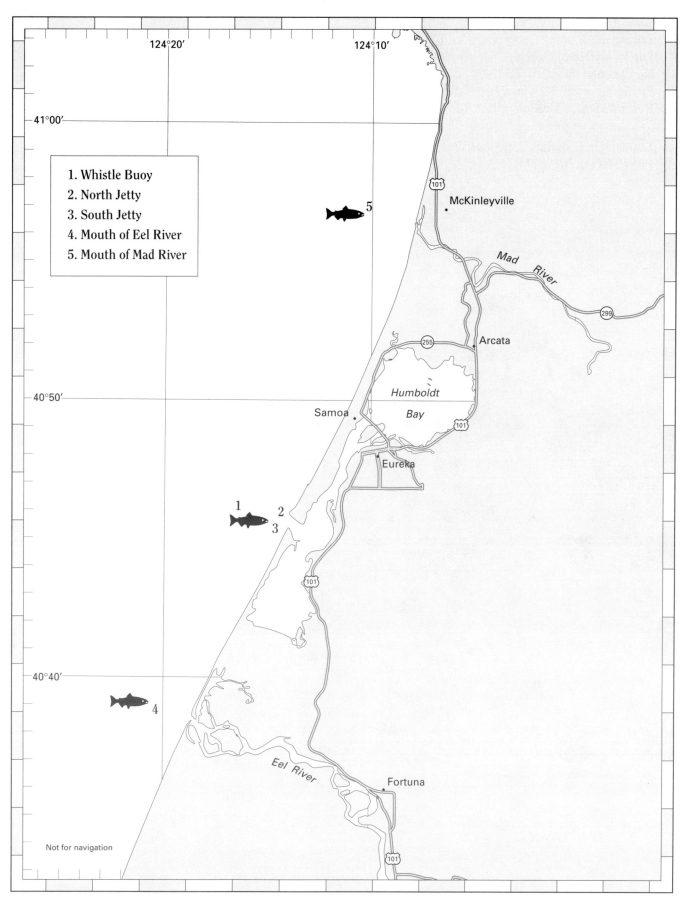

1. Whistle Buoy
2. North Jetty
3. South Jetty
4. Mouth of Eel River
5. Mouth of Mad River

41°00′

124°20′   124°10′

5

McKinleyville

Mad River

299

255

Arcata

Humboldt

40°50′

Samoa

Bay

101

Eureka

1   2
    3

101

40°40′

4

101

Eel River

Fortuna

101

Not for navigation

Map 7-16: Eureka–Humboldt Bay.

Bait and Tackle

Bucksports Sporting Goods, Eureka (707) 442-1832
Eureka Fly Shop, Eureka (707) 444-2000
New Outdoor Store, Arcata (707) 822-0321
Pro Sport Center, McKinleyville (707) 839-9445
Roger's Market, McKinleyville (707) 839-3866

Camping

Samoa Boat Launch, County Park (707) 445-7651
Eureka KOA (707) 822-4243

Michael Golden of Arcata with 20-pounder.

Trinidad *(See map 7.17 on next page)*

Hot spots

    CB Channel 11

    Information (707) 677-3625

    1. Little River

    2. 20-Fathom Line

    3. Trinidad Head

    4. Scotty Point

Geography

Trinidad Harbor is formed by the large, rocky outcropping of Trinidad Head (see Map 7.17). This large rock offers protection from the prevailing northwest winds and swells. Once you leave the harbor, you are in the open ocean.

This area, with its cold water and rocky reefs, attracts and holds large numbers of salmon, especially during the summer. Trinidad is still a significant commercial fishing port and was a major whaling center at one time. Trinidad is reached by taking Highway 101 about 25 miles north of Eureka.

Photo 7-28: A 10-pound salmon caught by Alfred Kuo.

Weather and Sea Conditions

This north coast port can be rough and dangerous, especially with winds and a large swell. Salmon fishing takes place outside the protection of Trinidad Head from one mile out to the 40-fathom line about 10 miles out. There is often fog during the summer. Most mornings are calm, until northwest winds kick up in the afternoon.

Fishing

The rich waters off Trinidad have historically been a magnet for large salmon. In the 1980's it was common for anglers to routinely catch three-fish limits of salmon weighing 100 pounds and more. Even with the greatly diminished stocks of salmon and reduced fishing season and limits, Trinidad still provides excellent salmon fishing.

Most salmon are caught by trolling, most of which is rather shallow for salmon, from 15 to 20 feet. At times the salmon are deeper, down to 150 feet, and fishermen with downriggers are able to reach them. Mooching is not very popular here, perhaps because the limit for king salmon is one fish per day.

Party Boats

One or more party boats are available through Bob's Boat Basin (707) 677-3625.

Bait and Tackle

    Salty's Sporting Goods, Trinidad (707) 677-3625

    Bob's Boat Basin, Trinidad Harbor (707) 677-3625

Launch Facilities

Bob's Boat Basin. The rail launch will accommodate most small boats, but it can be slow if many boats are waiting.

Camping

    Big Lagoon County Park (9 miles north of Trinidad on Highway 101)

    Patrick's Point State Park (6 miles north of Trinidad on Highway 101) (707)677-3570

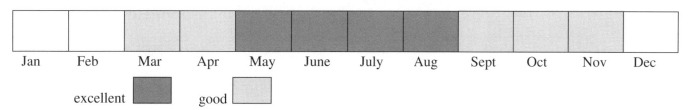

Diagram 7-13: Trinidad's best salmon-fishing months.

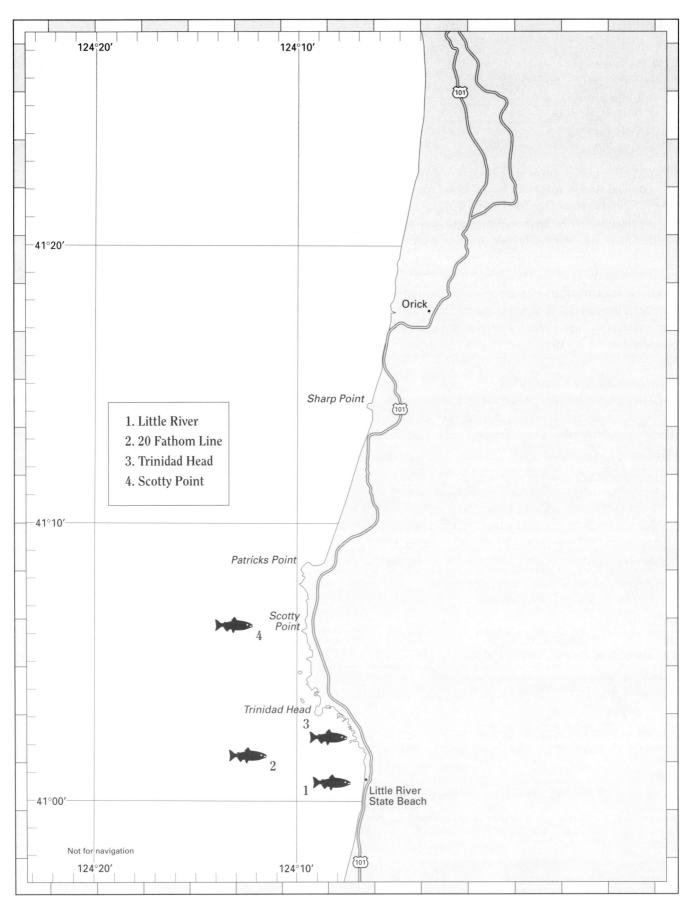

1. Little River
2. 20 Fathom Line
3. Trinidad Head
4. Scotty Point

Orick

Sharp Point

Patricks Point

Scotty Point

4

Trinidad Head

3

2

1

Little River
State Beach

Not for navigation

Map 7-17: Trinidad.

Crescent City *(See map 7.18 on next page)*

Hot spots

Information (707) 464-7687

1. Sister Rocks
2. Chase Ledge
3. Buoy 2
4. Point St. George

Geography

Crescent City, about 20 miles south of the Oregon border, is the northernmost fishing port in California (see Map 7.18). The many rocky pinnacles and reefs provide rich fishing areas that concentrate bait and salmon.

Weather and Sea Conditions

The well-protected harbor, with its extensive seawalls and the Point St. George headland providing protection from the prevailing northwest winds and swells, is a safe area for close-in fishing, usually within sight of the number 2 buoy. Like most of the north coast, offshore winds and swells can be dangerous. Fog is also often present during the summer.

Fishing

Crescent City offers safe access to the northernmost salmon waters of California. Salmon congregate in this area from May through September. Fishing starts right outside the harbor at the number 2 buoy. Most salmon are caught trolling, but some anglers are successful mooching.

Party Boats

Lindbrook Sportfishing, 101 Starfish Way, Crescent City 95531 (707) 464-7687

Harbor Charters, 128 Anchor Way, Crescent City 95531 (707) 464-2420

Bait and Tackle

Chart Room Marina, 130 Anchor Way, Crescent City 95531 (707) 464-5993

Crescent City Harbor, 101 Citizens' Dock Road, Crescent City 95531 (707) 464-6174

Sandie's Marine and Sport, Crescent City (707) 465-6499

Launch Facilities

Chart Room Marina has a 4-lane launch ramp.

Crescent City Harbor has an excellent launch ramp and hoist.

Camping

Bayside RV Park (707) 458-3321

Ramblin' Rose RV Resort (707) 4874831

Village Camper Inn (707) 464-3544

Jedediah Smith Redwood State Park (707) 464-9533

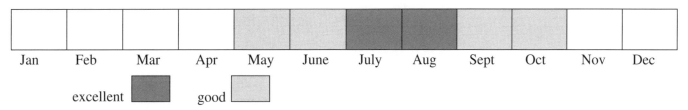

Diagram 7-14: Crescent City's best salmon-fishing months.

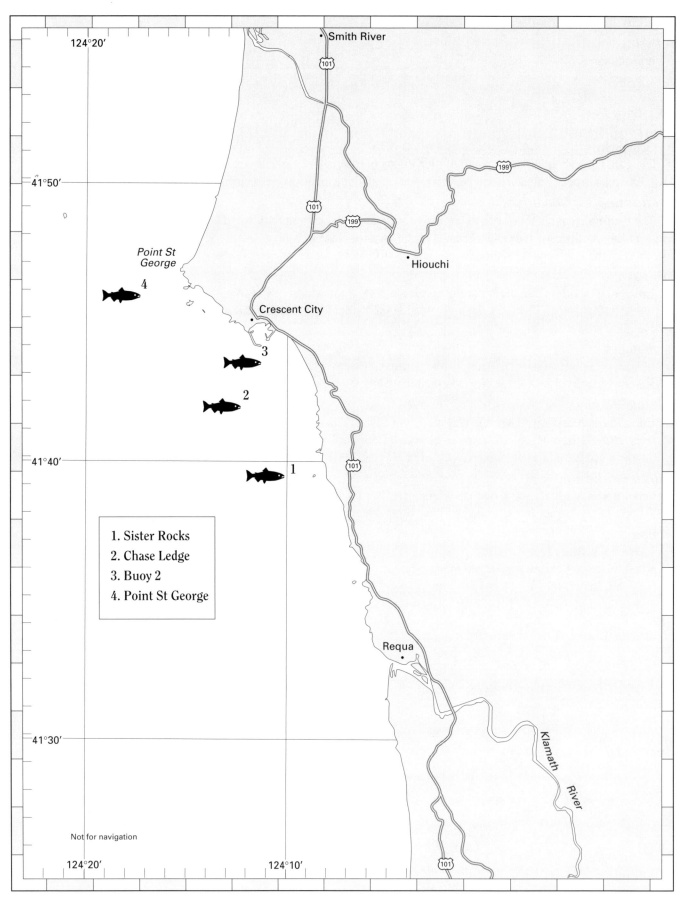

Map 7-18: Crescent City.

Chapter 8: Fishing for Salmon in Northern California Rivers

River Salmon-Fishing Techniques, 97 • Smith River, 98 • Klamath River, 98 • Trinity River, 102 • Eel River, 105 Sacramento River, 107

River Salmon-Fishing Techniques

When salmon enter fresh water, they tend to stop eating and concentrate on their main purpose in life: to spawn. Their stomachs shrink and their gonads enlarge in preparation for spawning. Males develop a hooked jaw, and their colors darken. At this time, salmon become aggressive and will attack any shiny, flashing, or vibrating lure, and they will also bite roe.

From shore, anglers can cast spinners or spoons slightly upstream and let them drift down with the current, retrieving them just fast enough to engage the blades and cause them to flutter. Or they can side-drift roe on the bottom, casting slightly upstream and letting the roe drift downstream into the river's deep holes (see Diagram 8-3 for rigging roe). Or they can cast a spinner or a large spin-'n-glo with a heavy weight into a hole or run and wait until a salmon strikes.

From boats, back-bouncing is popular (see Diagram 8-1); back-trolling is the same technique but using a lure. Position the boat upstream from a hole and slowly power it, facing upstream, and move from side to side, allowing the current to carry the boat and the trailing lines backward over the deepest and most productive parts of the hole. You can use roe in this technique. A lure with a sardine wrap is also often used—a fillet of sardine wrapped to the underside of the lure with a light monofilament line (see Diagram 8-2). The most popular lures are Flatfish (M-2, T-50, and T-55) and Quickfish.

In the Klamath and Trinity Rivers, tuna balls are popular. They are made from canned tuna wrapped in mesh and tied into $^3/_4$- to 1-inch balls. The ball is attached to a hook and drifted through deep holes and

Photo 8-1: A 45-pound Smith River salmon caught by Michael Golden.

Northern California Rivers: Smith, Klamath, Trinity, Eel, and Sacramento Rivers

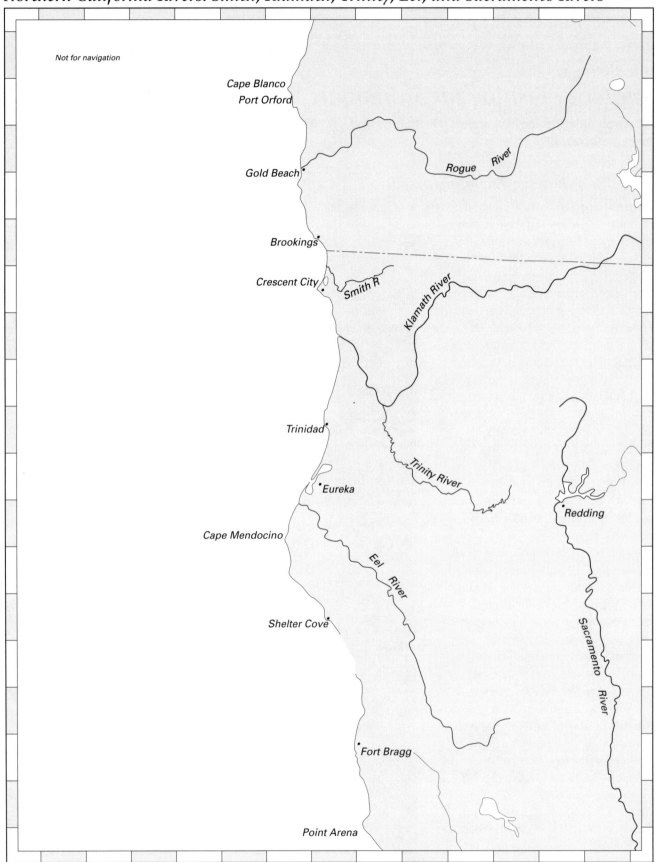

Map 8-1: Northern California salmon-fishing rivers.

runs. (Roe can be used this way, too [see Diagram 8-3]. Place a quarter-sized ball of roe in a mesh bag, tie the bag, and put the hook through the bag. Or snell a hook with a bait loop and place a quarter-size ball of roe under the bait loop.)

Northern California Rivers: Smith, Klamath, Trinity, Eel, and Sacramento Rivers

Smith River

Geography

The Smith River is the northernmost salmon river in California, almost at the Oregon border. It produces some very large salmon—with 40- to 60-pounders caught every year. It is a wild river with no dams and a fairly intact natural rainforest that catches and absorbs the heavy rains. The river clears quickly, often in a day or two after a storm.

Fishing

Salmon start entering the Smith in September and continue through March. November and December are the best months for larger salmon.

Fishing on the Smith is done mostly by drift boats that back-troll plugs or back-bounce roe. Shore fishermen drift roe, spoons, or spinners, or cast out with a heavy weight and let a spinner work in the current.

The most popular bank fishing spots are Bailey Hole, Rooney Hole, Early Hole, and Hiouchi Hole. Boat fishing is done from the confluence of the middle and south forks downstream. The whole 15 miles is navigable. The most popular launching sites are at the South Park and Jedediah Smith State Park. Takeouts are at Smith River Outfitters and Rowdy Creek.

Camping

Jedediah Smith State Park (707) 458-3310
Hiouchi Hamlet RV Resort (707) 458-3321

Guides

Gordy's Guide Service (707) 442-8904
Smith River Outfitters (707) 487-0935
John Woolworth Guide Service (707) 487-7571
Greg Nico Guide Service (707) 464-7320
Lunker Fish Trips (800) 248-4704
Bear Ridge Fishing Company (707) 539-9534
Steelie Dan's Guide Service (916) 684-7148

Klamath River

Geography

The Klamath River is more than 200 miles long and flows from Oregon to the mouth near the town of

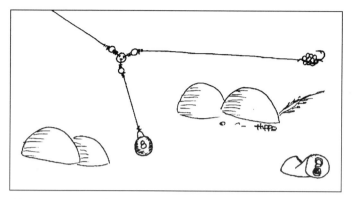

Diagram 8-1: Back-bouncing is an effective method for getting the bait on the bottom of deep holes where salmon congregate.

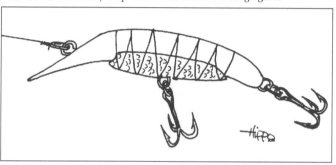

Diagram 8-2: A sardine wrap for back-trolling lures, such as Flatfish or Quickfish.

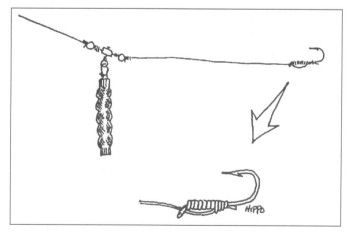

Diagram 8-3: A bait loop with roe. The loop is a quick and easy way to put roe on the hook. This rig is used for side-drifting in rivers.

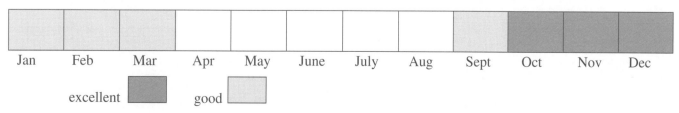

Jan	Feb	Mar	Apr	May	June	July	Aug	Sept	Oct	Nov	Dec

excellent ▢   good ▢

Diagram 8-1: Smith River's best salmon-fishing months.

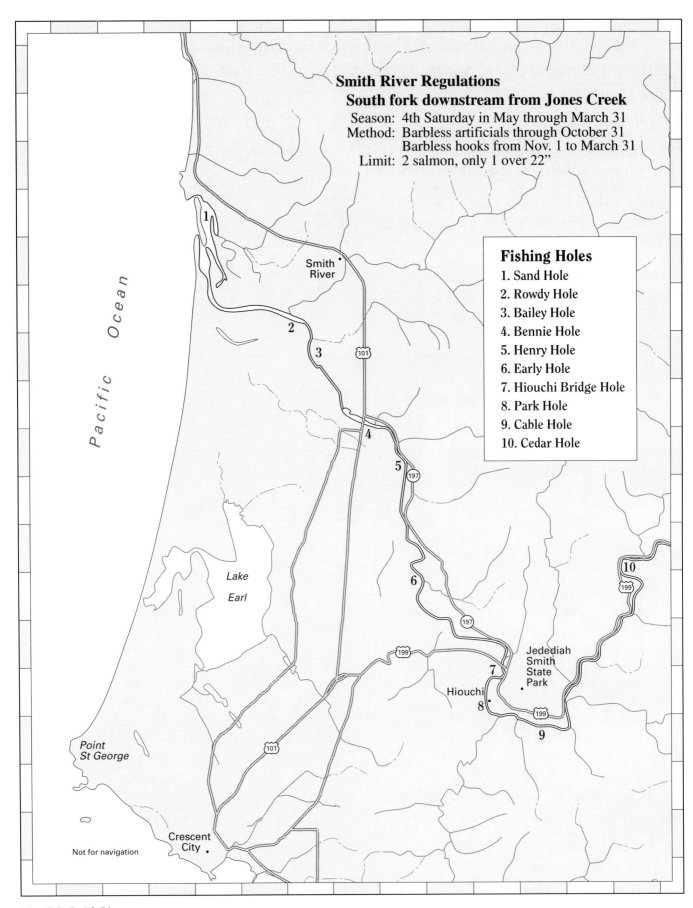

Smith River Regulations
South fork downstream from Jones Creek
Season: 4th Saturday in May through March 31
Method: Barbless artificials through October 31
Barbless hooks from Nov. 1 to March 31
Limit: 2 salmon, only 1 over 22"

Fishing Holes
1. Sand Hole
2. Rowdy Hole
3. Bailey Hole
4. Bennie Hole
5. Henry Hole
6. Early Hole
7. Hiouchi Bridge Hole
8. Park Hole
9. Cable Hole
10. Cedar Hole

Map 8-2: Smith River.

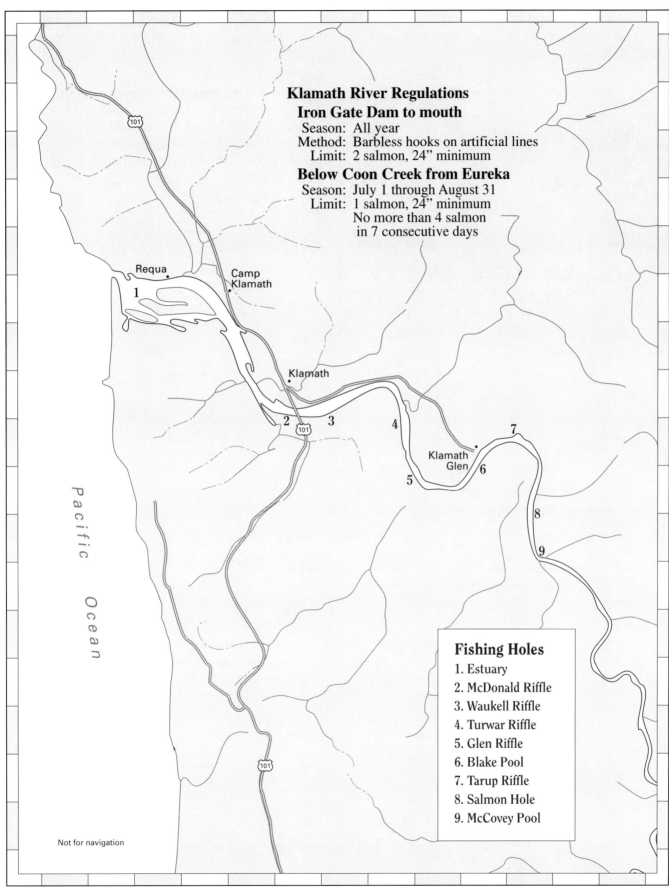

Klamath River Regulations
Iron Gate Dam to mouth
Season: All year
Method: Barbless hooks on artificial lines
Limit: 2 salmon, 24" minimum
Below Coon Creek from Eureka
Season: July 1 through August 31
Limit: 1 salmon, 24" minimum
No more than 4 salmon
in 7 consecutive days

Requa

Camp
Klamath

1

Klamath

2   3   4

Klamath
Glen   7

5   6

8

9

Pacific Ocean

Fishing Holes
1. Estuary
2. McDonald Riffle
3. Waukell Riffle
4. Turwar Riffle
5. Glen Riffle
6. Blake Pool
7. Tarup Riffle
8. Salmon Hole
9. McCovey Pool

Not for navigation

Map 8-3: Klamath River.

Klamath about 20 miles south of Crescent City. The run of salmon is improving after being severely depressed during the 1980's. Strict management and improved climatic conditions have helped the run rebound. The salmon are more heavily fished in the lower reaches of the river.

Photo 8-2: Greg Goddard bank fishing on the Klamath River.

Fishing

Salmon start entering the Klamath River in late August and September, and fish are caught through December. In the lower river, boats troll spoons and spinners. Bank anglers use spinners on spoons. The most popular fishing spots are in the tidal waters of the estuary below Requa, at Camp Klamath, and above and below the Highway 101 Bridge.

Camping

Camper Corral (707) 482-5741
Camp Klamath RV Park (707) 482-3405
Redwood Rest Resort (707) 482-5033
Oak Bottom (530) 241-6584
Riverside RV Park (707) 482-2523
Elk Creek Campground (916) 493-2208

Guides

Gordy's Guide Service (707) 442-8904
Seiad Valley Guide Service (916) 496-3291

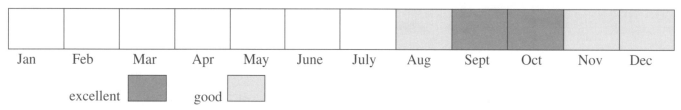

| Jan | Feb | Mar | Apr | May | June | July | Aug | Sept | Oct | Nov | Dec |

excellent ▧   good ▨

Diagram 8-2: Klamath River's best salmon-fishing months.

Steelie Dan's Guide Service (916) 684-7148
Bear Ridge Fishing Company (707) 539-9534
Northern California Guide Service (530) 527-9584

Trinity River

Geography

The Trinity River is actually a fork of the Klamath River and joins it near Weitchpec. It was dammed in the 1960's to make Trinity Lake above Lewiston. The river flows through largely gravel beds and because of the dam, it often remains clear even after rainstorms. Highway 299 runs along the river and provides great access.

Fishing

The annual salmon run begins in September and lasts through December.

Salmon average 9 to 12 pounds in the Trinity. Bank access is very good, and any of the deep holes will hold salmon during a run. The most popular holes are Willow Creek, Burnt Ranch Falls, the South Fork, Hawkins Bar, Gray Falls, Cedar Flat, Big Ben, Helena, and Junction City.

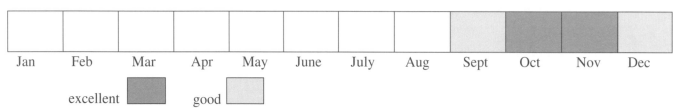

| Jan | Feb | Mar | Apr | May | June | July | Aug | Sept | Oct | Nov | Dec |

excellent ▧   good ▨

Diagram 8-3: Trinity River's best salmon-fishing months.

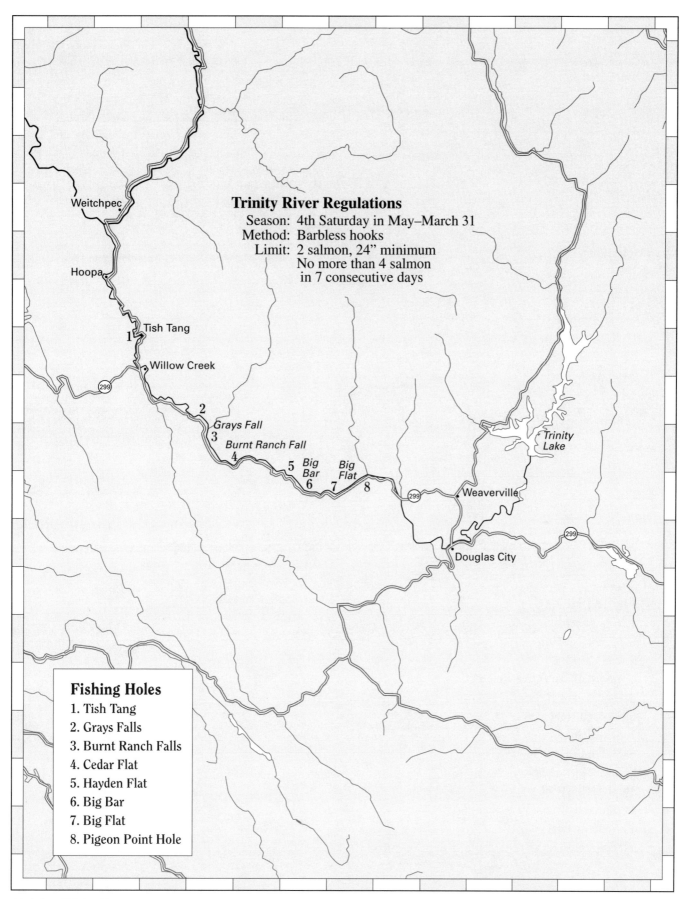

Trinity River Regulations

Season: 4th Saturday in May–March 31
Method: Barbless hooks
Limit: 2 salmon, 24" minimum
No more than 4 salmon
in 7 consecutive days

Fishing Holes

1. Tish Tang
2. Grays Falls
3. Burnt Ranch Falls
4. Cedar Flat
5. Hayden Flat
6. Big Bar
7. Big Flat
8. Pigeon Point Hole

Map 8-4: Trinity River.

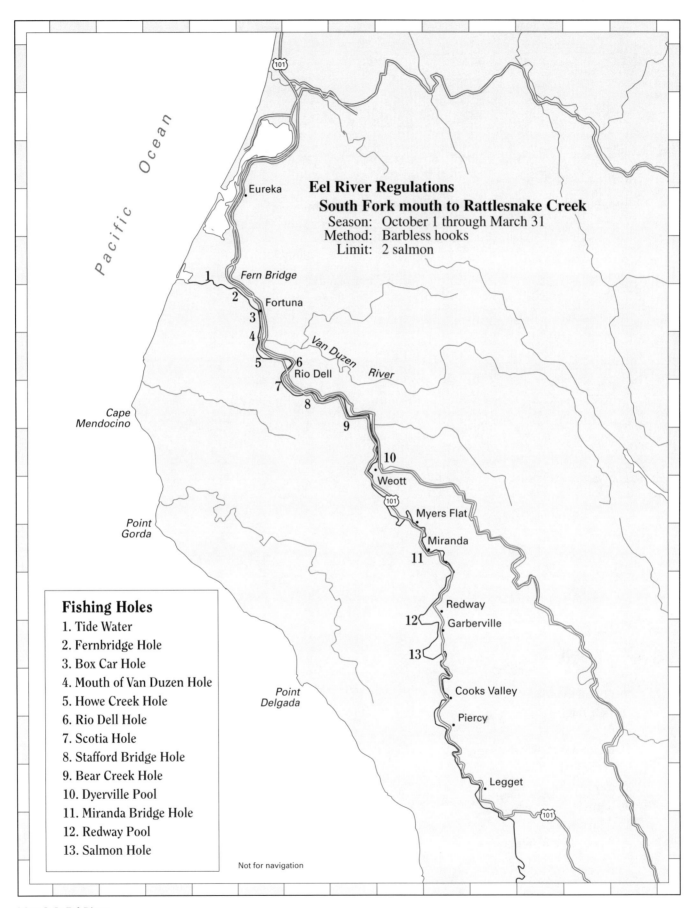

Eel River Regulations
South Fork mouth to Rattlesnake Creek
Season: October 1 through March 31
Method: Barbless hooks
Limit: 2 salmon

Fishing Holes
1. Tide Water
2. Fernbridge Hole
3. Box Car Hole
4. Mouth of Van Duzen Hole
5. Howe Creek Hole
6. Rio Dell Hole
7. Scotia Hole
8. Stafford Bridge Hole
9. Bear Creek Hole
10. Dyerville Pool
11. Miranda Bridge Hole
12. Redway Pool
13. Salmon Hole

Not for navigation

Map 8-5: Eel River.

The Trinity can also be fished by drift boat. Popular methods of fishing are drifting roe and tuna balls as well as casting spinners or spoons. Boat anglers often will pull plugs, such as Flatfish or Quickfish (see Diagrams 8-1 and 8-2).

Camping

Grays Falls Campground (707) 442-1721
Hayden Flat Campground (530) 246-5112
Big Flat Campground (530) 246-5112
Cedar Stock Resort (800) 982-2279
Bigfoot Campgrounds (800) 422-5219
Trinity River RV Park and Campground
(916) 623-3964

Guides

Gordy's Guide Service (707) 442-8904
Gerry Gray (888) 286-7250
John Rickey's Guide Service (530) 244-2494
Steelie Dan's Guide Service (916) 684-7148
God's Country Guide Service (916) 266-3297
Bear Ridge Fishing Company (707) 539-9534

Eel River

Geography

The Eel River runs along Highway 101 and is fishable from Leggett, South Fork of the mouth to where it empties, into the main stem of the Eel near Weott. The main stem of the Eel is fishable

Photo 8-3: The Eel River above Garberville.

all the way to the mouth. Heavy storms will raise the river and blow it out for a week or more before it becomes fishable. The Eel runs through some beautiful country, including many redwood groves.

Fishing

The Eel River provides some fine salmon fishing from September through December. Salmon average 10 to 15 pounds with some 20- and 30-pounders taken. The peak time is usually November.

Bank fishermen throw spinners and spoons or drift roe. Drift boat fishermen usually side-drift roe, but some pull plugs. Popular fishing spots are Leggett, Piercy, Cooks Valley, Richardson Grove, Garberville, Redway Bridge, Deans Creek, Phillipsville, Miranda, Myers Flat, Weott, Pepperwood, and Scotia.

Camping

Albee Creek Campground (707) 946-2409
Standish Hickey State Recreation Area (707) 925-6482
Benbow Lake State Recreation Area (707) 923-3238
Benbow Valley RV Resort (707) 923-2777
Richardson Grove State Park (707) 247-3318

Guides

Steelie Dan's Guide Service (916) 684-7148
Bear Ridge Fishing Company (707) 539-9534
Northern California Guide Service (530) 527-9584

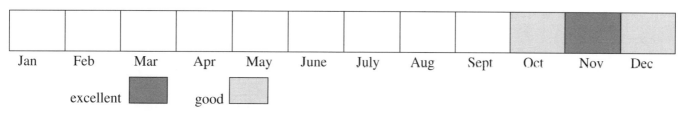

| Jan | Feb | Mar | Apr | May | June | July | Aug | Sept | Oct | Nov | Dec |

excellent ▮   good ▯

Diagram 8-4: Eel River's best salmon-fishing months.

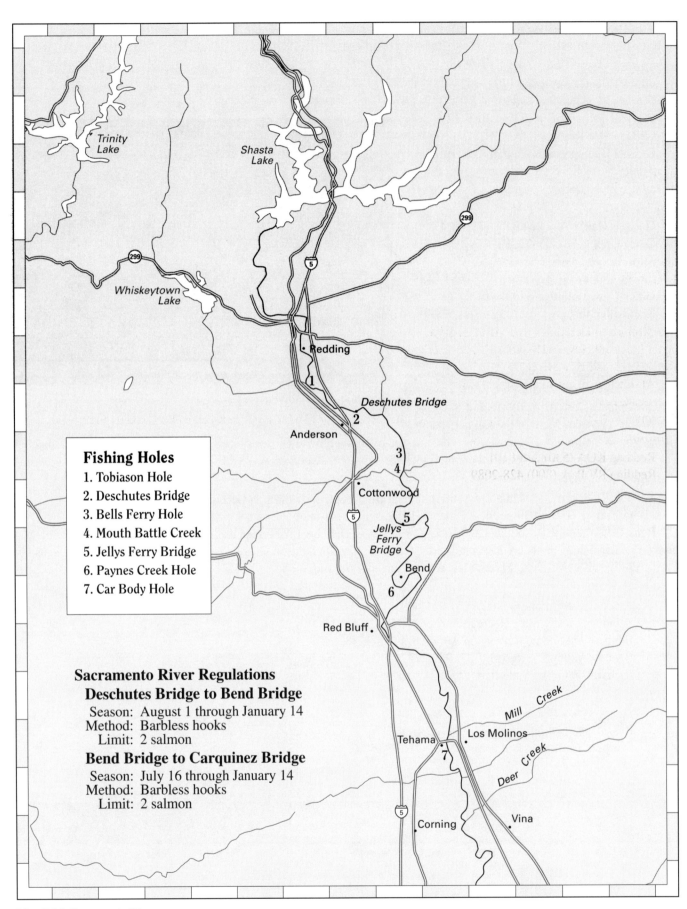

Fishing Holes

1. Tobiason Hole
2. Deschutes Bridge
3. Bells Ferry Hole
4. Mouth Battle Creek
5. Jellys Ferry Bridge
6. Paynes Creek Hole
7. Car Body Hole

Sacramento River Regulations

Deschutes Bridge to Bend Bridge

Season: August 1 through January 14
Method: Barbless hooks
  Limit: 2 salmon

Bend Bridge to Carquinez Bridge

Season: July 16 through January 14
Method: Barbless hooks
  Limit: 2 salmon

Map 8-16: Sacramento River.

Sacramento River

Geography

The Sacramento River provides the main run of king salmon in California, averaging 500,000 fish a year. It drains from the Sierras and runs from Lake Shasta above Redding to the San Francisco Bay.

Fishing

Most of the salmon fishing is done from boats, because the river is wide and deep and the deep holes where salmon hold are difficult to reach from the shore. Back-trolling and back-bouncing roe are the most popular techniques. Guides are available, and novices should not try navigating new areas of the river without an experienced guide.

Photo 8-4: Four salmon from the Sacramento River.

Salmon are in the Sacramento River year round, but the season is only from July to January; it is closed from January to June to protect spawning salmon, especially the endangered winter-run king salmon.

The main fishing on the Sacramento River is from Los Molinos to Deschutes Road Bridge. Some of the better holes are Howe's Hole, Ball's Ferry Hole, Barge Hole, Bend, and Bow River.

At times there can also be good fishing on the American, Feather, and Yuba Rivers, which run into the Sacramento River. Unlike the Sacramento, these three rivers offer good fishing from the bank as well as from boats.

Camping

Redding KOA (530) 246-0101
Redding RV Park (800) 428-2089
Sacramento River RV Park (530) 365-6402
Driftwood Fishing Resort (916) 384-2851
Balls Ferry Fishing Resort (916) 365-2224

Guides

Steelie Dan's Guide Service (916) 684-7148
Northern California Guide Service (530) 527-9584
Iron Canyon Outfitters (888) 443-4748
Smith River Outfitters (707)487-0935
Bob's Guide Service (539) 222-8058
Sacramento Sport Fishing Guides (916) 487-3392
Rick Soto Fishing Guide (916) 226-0888
Free Willy's Guide Service (916) 529- 1233
M. L. Pound's Guide Service (916) 529-1233
Bear Ridge Fishing Company (707) 539-9534
Mike Bogue's Guide Service (916) 246-8457

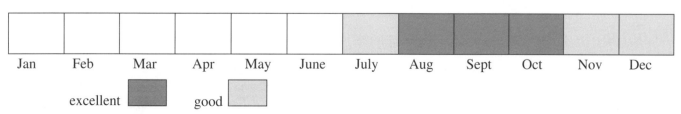

Diagram 8-5: Sacramento River's best salmon-fishing months.

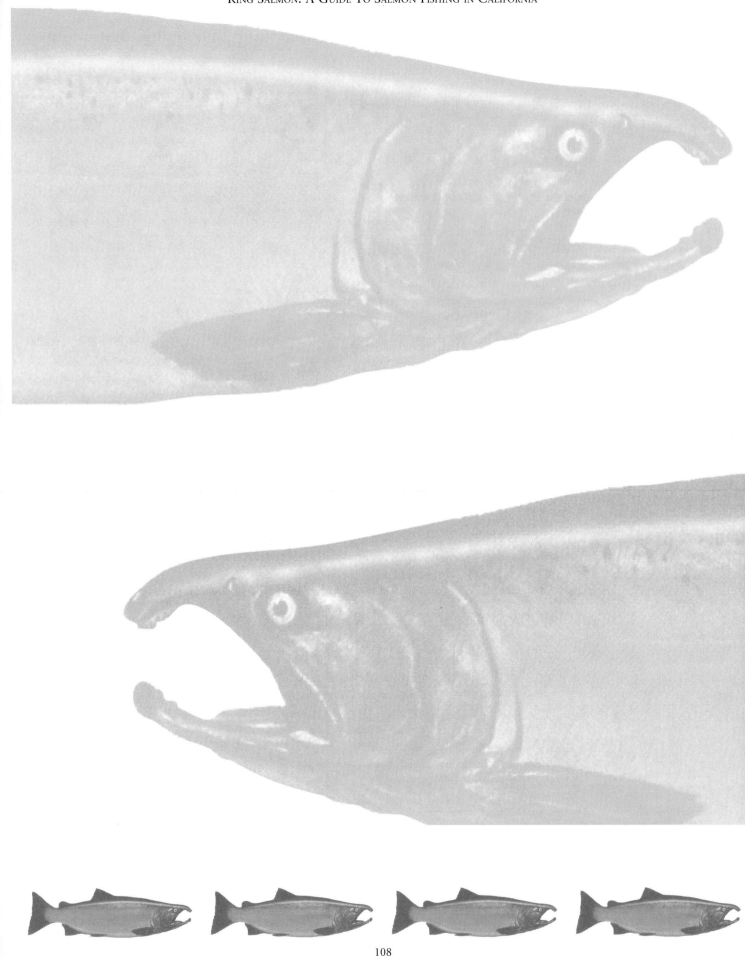

Chapter 9: Natural History

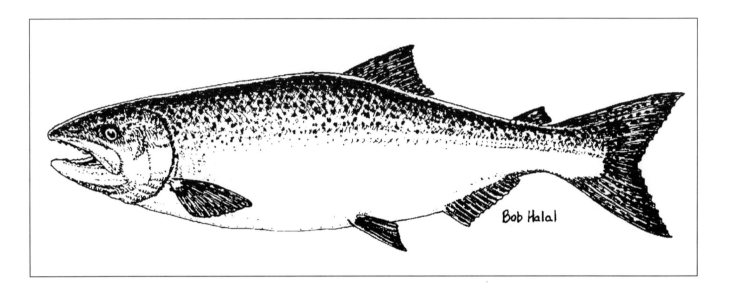

Bob Halal

"When we entered the rivers, compelled by the sacred, fatal urgings of our loins, a huge wave preceded us to let the hunters know we were coming. The rivers swelled and the fishermen roared with glee at our spirit churning the water to foam."
—Queen Salmon, David Simpson and Jane Lapiner

The king salmon is also known as the Chinook or the tyee. Its scientific name is Oncorhynchus tshawytscha. There is little fossil history of the salmon. The only salmon know before the Pleistocene Age is probably a relative of the smelt, but the Pleistocene fossils are fragmentary and not very helpful. It is generally agreed that the salmon family must have attained its present distribution during and partly as a result of the succession of ice ages in Pleistocene and more recent times. All salmon arose from a common ancestor not later than the beginning of the Pleistocene Age, over half a million years ago.

It is not known whether the common ancestor of the salmon was of marine or freshwater origin. It possibly could have come from the brackish waters of estuaries. Today, salmon are able to live in both fresh water and salt water, as well as brackish environments.

The Salmon Life Cycle

"We were royalty visiting from a larger, more exotic realm, charging each valley from Siberia to Point Conception with the power of the deep, and the exaltation of purest sex. And when that was over, our carcasses sent to the peaks a stench that sickened even the skunk people, but spoke of oceanic riches being returned to the rivers, and the land, to put spine in the green growth and recharge the cycle of life. We were the mortar and thong that bound river and ocean, land and sea. We were the lifebringers."
—Queen Salmon, David Simpson and Jane Lapiner

After one to six years at sea, salmon locate their home river by scent. They also are able to migrate by using the magnetic fields of the earth, which they sense with an organ in their head. In their home river, they spawn. Some spawning runs are more complicated than others. In some rivers, they occur every month of the year, and each month, it is a different group destined for a different tributary or portion of the main river.

King salmon usually spawn in the late spring or early summer, but there are also fall and winter runs. Salmon may spawn just above high tide or travel long distances—as far as 2,000 miles up the Yukon River. The young may either go to sea during their first year of life or remain one or even two years in the stream. These young salmon grow rapidly in the sea and mature in three to eight years, usually in four or five.

All king salmon die after mating. Spawned-out salmon will often be seen barely swimming around in the river, their bodies covered with white spots of fungus and their fins falling off. After the salmon spawn, the stench of their rotting flesh can be smelled along the river's spawning areas. But the dead and decaying carcasses provide nutrients for the streamside habitat and for the river itself. Dead and dying salmon provide food for ravens, buzzards, coyotes, and other animals that feed on carrion, as well as many bacteria and the insects on which newborn salmon survive. The death of the salmon after spawning gives rebirth to perpetuate the cycle of life.

The king salmon's life cycle begins sometime between July and November in the shallow water of streams where the water is clean and the bottom is gravel (for the salmon life cycle, see Diagram 9-2). There the mother buries the fertilized eggs in a nest several inches deep or a foot deep and 12 feet long, called a "redd." When hatched—in 7 to 12 weeks—the young fish, called "alevins," emerge into the water between the stones. Their yolk sacs are attached to the underside of their bodies, and they feed on these yolk sacs as they develop in the gravel for several weeks. They move freely as their yolk sacs get smaller. Eventually, the young salmon make their way above the surface of the gravel. Their yolk sacs disappear completely. Now they are called fry, or fingerlings, and are about 1 inch long. Feeding and growing,

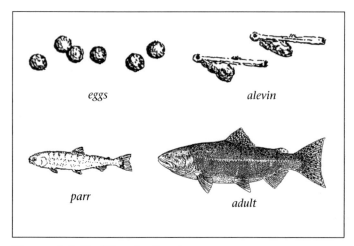

eggs   *alevin*

parr   *adult*

Diagram 9-2: The life cycle of a salmon.

they disperse into the stream.

In the next stage in the life cycle, the fingerling becomes a parr when it reaches a length longer than a person's finger. Parr have a series of dark blotches on their side that look like thumbprints.

After a year or more in fresh water, avoiding predators and feeding mostly on aquatic insect life, the parr is ready to go to sea. On its scales, a substance called "guanine" has been deposited, hiding its parr marks and giving it a shiny silvery appearance. It is now called a "smolt." During the late fall or winter, it will wait for the flooding rivers and streams to give it the fast currents it needs to reach the sea, where it will feed in the rich waters of the ocean. (The alevin-parr-smolt process is concluded in a few months in some rivers, and lasts as long as two years in others.)

King salmon feeding in the rich waters off the Gulf of the Farallones are said to grow 1 inch a month. When caught, they average less than 10 pounds, but 20-pounders are common, 30-pounders are nice trophies, and each year a 40+-pounder is landed. The majority of sport-caught salmon in the Gulf of the Farallones measure from 20 to 26 inches and weigh from 4 to 5 pounds up to about 10 pounds. A commercially netted Alaskan king salmon was said to have weighed 126 pounds and measured 4 feet 10 inches long. The latest angling record is a 93-pounder in 1977.

The Salmon's Habitat

A king salmon's ocean range is from northern Japan to southern California or even farther. In 1995, a 19-pound king salmon was landed in Ensenada, Baja California, about 75 miles south of the California border.

Salmon follow the currents and forage fish and shrimp in the offshore waters of the Pacific. Sardines, which used to range in massive schools from southern California to northern California, were once a main food source for king salmon (for a map of salmon migration from Oregon to California, see Map 9-1). Kings all the way from British Columbia converged on the shores of central California to feed on sardines, starting in southern California, as far down as Newport Beach, and followed them up to Santa Barbara, San Luis Obispo, and Monterey. The overfishing and disappearance of

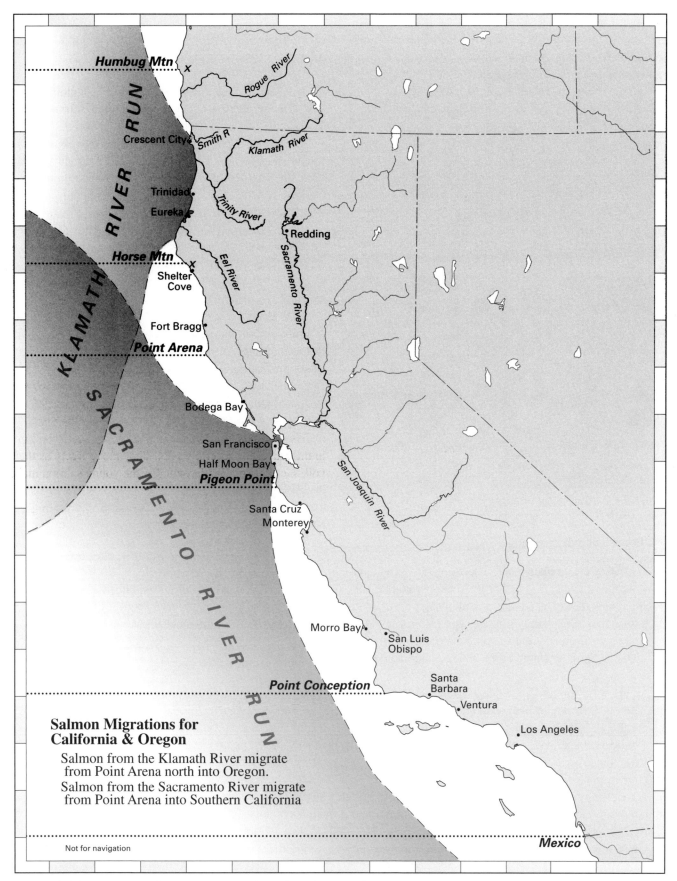

Map 9-1: California/Oregon salmon migrations. Salmon from the Klamath River migrate from Point Arena north into Oregon. Salmon from the Sacramento River migrate from Point Arena south into Southern California.

sardines greatly changed salmon migrations because they limited its food supply.

Another important source of food for the salmon is the anchovy. Large schools of anchovies abound in the waters off California. In late June or early July, anchovies make their spawning runs off the beaches of California. The salmon usually soon follow to feed on the anchovies.

In the early spring, another food source, baby rock cod, from 1 to 3 inches long, comes to the surface, often congregating in the rocky areas near the Farallon Islands. Here, the salmon gorge themselves and grow fatter.

Photo 9-2: A Native American carving of a salmon.

Photo 9-1: Squid are a favorite food of salmon.

Squid are also a favorite food of salmon. Squid are often thick around the Monterey Bay, and the salmon feed there for long periods. But squid also congregate in offshore waters all along the Pacific Coast, and salmon will feed on them at any time.

Krill, or small shrimp, which abound in the Gulf of the Farallones, are another favorite food for the king salmon. They will feed on schools of krill for weeks at a time. Salmon that have been feeding on krill have bright red meat that is extremely tasty.

The salmon taken south of Point Arena are mainly from the Sacramento River drainage, but they may come from as far north as British Columbia and the Columbia River of Washington and Oregon. Sacramento River fish also range as far south as Southern California and as far north as British Columbia. Salmon north of Point Arena are mainly from the Klamath River.

There is some mystery as to exactly where the salmon go during their stay in the ocean. Some salmon are said to be caught by the high-seas driftnet fleet fishing far offshore. And during warm currents, such as El Niño, the salmon seem to disappear, returning to spawn only after they disappear.

Native Americans and Salmon

"We were so many once. The sea itself would churn with the wake of our endless schools. When we turned in our great gyres, the head of the school would be half way down to Kodiak while our tail would still be deep in Siberian waters, pecked at by Aleut hunters brave enough to pursue us in flimsy skin boats. From frigid Kamchatka to the balmy southern coasts, we were known as the providers, who guaranteed meat to bear and sable, and raven and human and a multitude of others."
—Queen Salmon, David Simpson and Jane Lapiner

All the way from the tip of Alaska down to Northern California, Native American Indians had a close relationship with salmon. The rivers where salmon spawned provided enough food to sustain rich cultures with a division of labor. This wealth allowed for leisure time and for the division of society into specialized functions, such as priests, artists, canoe builders, fisherman, weavers and others. These cultures had well-developed societies and traded with each other up and down the coast in their seagoing canoes.

They respected the salmon as part of the natural cycle that enabled them to provide enough food to sustain them throughout the year. They developed the technology to preserve salmon through drying, smoking, and burying it in the ground to provide the delicacy of aged salmon. The salmon provided a bounty during the season when it was fresh. When preserved, it provided protein for the rest of the year. Dried and smoked salmon was traded with inland tribes.

These Northwest Coast cultures reached all the way down into Northern California at the Klamath River, the only river in California that allowed a year-round culture to develop because of the amount of salmon it provided, along with a climate and geography that provided other bounties of nature—animals for hunting and roots, vegetables, fruits, and nuts for gathering (see Map 9-2 for California salmon tribes). A river where the salmon spawned was necessary for the development of these cultures because the amount of salmon necessary to feed a large developed society for a year could be taken only through the technology of using nets. The nets were made with fibers and strung across the river to take large amounts of salmon during their spawning run. This huge bounty of salmon could not be eaten fresh, so it had to be preserved through smoking and drying. These societies also took salmon from the ocean, where salmon were abundant year-round. They used seagoing canoes to troll and mooch for salmon.

Tribes south of the Klamath River fished for salmon but did not set up developed societies based around the salmon. They were hunter-gatherers who took salmon only during the seasons when the fish came up the rivers. They often made special trips to the areas where the salmon would be at certain times of the year and take a large quantity and dry and smoke what they could not eat fresh. All the rivers from San Francisco to the Klamath River carried runs of salmon. Even the tributaries of the San Joaquin and Sacramento Rivers that drained into San Francisco Bay had tremendous runs of salmon. The Indians on these rivers would take them at certain times of the year for their needs.

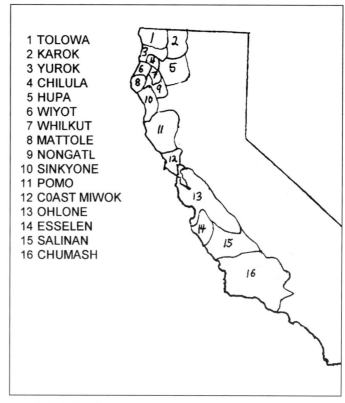

1 TOLOWA
2 KAROK
3 YUROK
4 CHILULA
5 HUPA
6 WIYOT
7 WHILKUT
8 MATTOLE
9 NONGATL
10 SINKYONE
11 POMO
12 COAST MIWOK
13 OHLONE
14 ESSELEN
15 SALINAN
16 CHUMASH

Map 9-2: California's salmon tribes.

Native American Fishing Techniques

Native American Indians used many techniques to net fish. The most common method was to stretch a net across a large part of a river during a spawning run and gill-net the salmon as they swam upstream. Often these nets were strung out across the river for many hours or even overnight. The mesh of the net was large enough for a salmon's head to get through but not the body; the salmon was trapped by the gills in its neck. The Indians then hauled the net full of salmon onto the bank or into a boat.

Other techniques of netting were also used. One was dip netting. The Indians would take long-handled nets and stand over a rock or other out-perch overlooking a river as the salmon went upstream to spawn. As the salmon swam by, they would dip out the salmon and haul them in one at a time. Another technique was a weir, or fish trap, that channeled the salmon going up the river into a small chute, from which they could be easily netted or captured in a pen.

Native American Indians also developed a method of trolling for salmon. For a weight, they used a large round rock, about the size of a grapefruit, and either put a groove around the outside or drill a hole in it to fasten a 20- to 25-foot rope made of local fibers to go over the edge of the canoe. Attached to this long rope was another piece of twine or fishing line to which they attached a baited hook made out of bones or antlers or a hook and a carved lure (most often out of an abalone shell in the shape of a small fish) that wobbled in the water. They trolled these lines behind their seagoing canoes, and when a salmon bit the bait or lure, they pulled the line into the canoe by hand. This is basically the same technique used by sport fishermen and commercial fishermen today to troll for salmon.

The Indians also developed mooching. They drifted in their canoes, dangling a line with a lure or baited hook below the boat. To attract the salmon, they jiggled the line up and down with the lure (most often, again, an abalone shell carved into the oblong shape of a spoon, or "fish") with a hook attached. When the salmon bit the hook, they pulled the line in, and pulled the salmon in by hand.

The Significance of Salmon for Native American Indians

Native American Indians saw the salmon as part of the cycle of nature: Salmon gave their life to go upstream to spawn and perpetuate the cycle. Native Americans worshiped salmon as the symbol of procreation and perpetuation of life. Salmon symbolized the basic necessity of perpetuating the species, of re-creating the next generation. Not only did salmon repeat their swim upstream to spawn every year, but their behavior was deeply rooted in the cycles of the earth.

The first rains in the fall filled the rivers, providing enough water for the salmon to enter from the ocean.

The cycle of the salmon spawning season is tied to all life in nature. As they ascend the rivers, they provide sustenance to many forms of animal and plant life. Sea lions and seals intercept the salmon as they enter the rivers and take a large amount to provide an important food source during certain parts of the year. Bears use the salmon swimming upstream as a source of protein to fatten up for the winter. They flock to the rivers and streams during the spawning season to take the salmon as they fight their way up the shallows and rapids toward their spawning waters. After the salmon spawn and die, they provide sustenance for eagles, ravens, vultures, and many other animals that eat the remains of the dead salmon streamside. The decomposing bodies of the salmon put back nutrients into the river and into the ground around the river to provide sustenance for the plants and aquatic life that, in turn, sustain the new generation of salmon hatched from the eggs. The salmon are entwined in the life cycle of the river, important to humans, bears, sea lions, even insects, and they provide the basis in the food chain for the small salmon fry to survive and make the next generation.

Native American Indians understood that without the salmon there would be no people, there would be no bears, no eagles, no sea lions; there would be no life. To the American Indian, salmon were the basis of the cycle of nature that provides life for all of us. That is why Native Americans worshipped salmon as a key part of the life cycle of nature.

Native Americans from Alaska down to the Klamath River had highly developed cultures that revolved around salmon. But other Native American tribes, all the way south to the Chumash of Santa Barbara, used salmon and respected them highly. And the Indians of the Sierras used the salmon that made their spawning runs in the fall up the small streams and tributaries of the San Joaquin and Sacramento Rivers. They took salmon in these small streams, mostly by spearing them.

Native Americans and Salmon Today

Today, Native Americans are still intimately connected to salmon. In Alaska, many commercial fishermen are Native Americans. Many tribes have developed commercial fishing industries for salmon as well as fish farms to raise salmon for the commercial market.

Native Americans have fought for their traditional treaty-based fishing rights, and federal courts have upheld these rights. These decisions have angered many non-Native American Indians who see Indians as getting special favors to take salmon while the resource is becoming smaller and their take of the salmon is shrinking. They blame Indians for the worsening conditions of salmon. My opinion is that this is untrue: Native Americans historically have been the preservers of nature, have worshipped nature, and are not to blame for the demise of the salmon.

Native American tribes have a long-term interest in seeing that the salmon are saved and that salmon runs are restored to the best that they can be. In many areas, progressive anglers and commercial fishermen have united with Native American Indians to help restore the salmon runs. In order to make this a successful fight, we need to see that it is not the Indians, the commercial fishermen, nor the anglers who are destroying the salmon runs. The salmon runs are being destroyed because of other factors: pollution, dams, and logging practices that silt up the spawning beds. In addition, the shifting of water from the rivers to agriculture and development decreases the water flow and raises temperatures during critical periods of the year so that salmon fry cannot survive. Water is being taken from major spawning rivers, such as the Sacramento and San Joaquin Rivers, and shipped to Southern California to provide water for new housing, development, and irrigation. Pollution is being dumped into the rivers, bays and oceans. These concerns need to be addressed in order to restore the salmon runs.

Blaming Native Americans for taking salmon only serves to divide the groups that could find a solution to the problems affecting the salmon runs. Sports fishermen, commercial fishermen, Indian tribes, environmentalists, and people who love nature need to be united in order to save the salmon.

Chapter 10: The Future of Salmon

Drought, 115 • Hatcheries, 116 • Protection of the Environment, 117

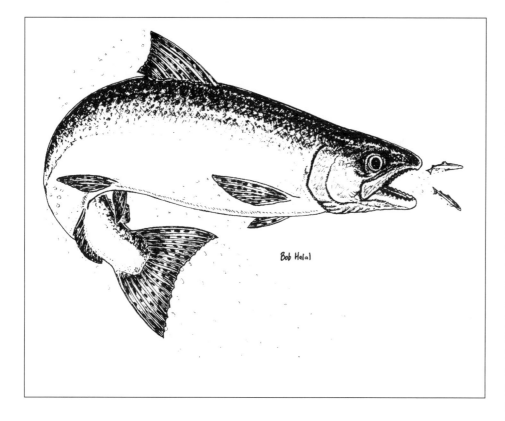

Bob Halal

"What has happened to the great howling storms of old, the fierce masses of water-laden air spinning with fury off the ocean? Always by November they would come. Brewed on the updrafts rising against the flanks of the Himalayas, and thrown north and east across all of Asia and out on the Gulf of Alaska. There was power! Deer, elk, even grizzly and human cowered in fear. The power of wind-driven sheets of rain shattering tops of ancient trees like so many dry sticks. The power surging in pregnant rivers hurtling themselves against banks, bursting open long-closed mouths. The power that again and again joined land and sea. Where is it now, that power? Gone with the giant trees, the grizzly, the salmon so huge that bear couldn't kill them?"

—Queen Salmon, David Simpson and Jane Lapiner

Drought

Drought severely reduces the ability of salmon to spawn and reproduce. With drought and without winter storms to raise the rivers, there is not enough water to wash out the sandbars that block the rivers from the ocean, and the salmon cannot make it upstream to spawn. The water of the winter rains and the rising of the rivers are needed to wash out the sandbars to the ocean and provide an entrance for the salmon to come upriver. The winter floods are also necessary to wash the silt off of the gravel to provide good spawning beds for the salmon. During periods of drought, salmon are not able to spawn in some rivers and in others are able to spawn only partially successfully.

There have always been droughts, and nature has equipped salmon to deal with them (see Diagram 10-1). Salmon can spend extra years in the ocean waiting for the years when the rains come and the rivers flow and they can make it upriver. They can also go into other rivers that have more water. In fact, some salmon always stray from their home river so that the species can protect itself against the home river not being able to sustain a spawn.

Salmon, unlike their cousin, the steelhead, spawn in the larger rivers, which usually have enough water to keep their mouths open and allow fish to enter. In drought years, however, there is not enough water for the salmon to get all the way upstream to the spawning gravels without encountering many dangers. Without high winter flows, they are subject to predation by sea lions at the mouth, to being caught in pools that become too warm, and to being delayed in arriving at their spawning grounds. If salmon are over-ripe, they cannot successfully spawn. Once at the spawning grounds, the waters may become too warm for their eggs to hatch without the cool water of winter flows, or the gravel may become too silted for the salmon to spawn or their eggs to survive if it is not cleaned by the high water of winter storms.

Storms and high winter flows are necessary not only for spawning but also for the other parts of the salmon life cycle. Salmon smolts, or the young salmon, need high winter flows to help wash them downstream into the ocean. During drought years, only a small percentage of young salmon make it to the ocean.

Summer is also a critical time in salmon rivers for the survival of the salmon. During the summer in drought years, some of the rivers stop flowing, and the water can become too hot to carry enough oxygen for the small salmon to survive. Then they can get trapped in small pools where herons and other birds can pick them off one by one. Warm water also encourages the growth of moss and algae, which also eat up oxygen.

In spite of all these natural obstacles, salmon have survived droughts over the millennia. Survival is built into their genes, and in fact, nature's droughts have probably helped make the species stronger. But nature's droughts are cyclical, not constant.

The Sacramento River winter run of king salmon has been listed as an endangered species since 1994. The population of winter-run Chinook (king) salmon has dropped by almost 99% over the past 25 years, hitting a low of 267 spawning adults in 1993—a dramatic drop from over 108,000 spawning adults in 1969.

Period	Length (years)	Average Runoff (MAF)
1579-82	4	12.4
1593-95	3	9.3
1618-20	3	13.2
1651-55	5	12.3
1719-24	6	12.6
1735-37	3	12.2
1755-61	6	13.3
1776-78	3	12.1
1793-95	3	10.7
1839-41	3	12.9
1843-46	4	12.3
1918-20 (actual)	3	12.0
1929-34 (actual)	6	9.8
1959-62 (actual)	4	13.0
1987-92 (actual)	6	10.0

Diagram 10-1: Droughts as indicated by tree rings. (Courtesy of the California Department of Fish and Game.)

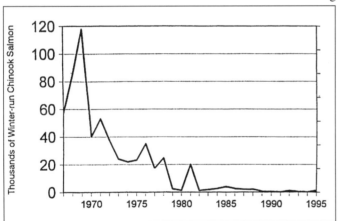

Diagram 10-2: Graph of Sacramento River winter-run Chinook salmon, 1967-1995. (Courtesy of the California Department of Fish and Game.)

Hatcheries

Fish hatcheries, which have been hailed as the cornerstone of the attempt to save the king salmon, are in fact causing wild salmon populations to become extinct. Although hatcheries were a major reason for the huge numbers of salmon caught in 1994 and 1995 off the coast of California, they are also contributing to the long-term decline of the species because they are genetically weaker than wild fish and are potential carriers of hatchery-related diseases, according to a three-year study requested by Congress by the National Research Council, an arm of the National Academy of Sciences.

Fish hatcheries were constructed to make up for spawning habitat lost after the building of dams. California has seven major hatcheries intended to produce salmon to supplement wild stocks. They are supposed to lessen the pressure on the wild populations of salmon while giving sportsmen, commercial fishermen, and American Indians fish to catch. But even though large numbers of hatchery-reared salmon have caused record catches, most officials now agree that wild salmon must still be protected and their spawning habitat improved.

It is not enough to merely have a large number of salmon. The long-term survival of the species depends on a rich store of genetic diversity, which will be lost if hatchery fish overwhelm the natural salmon stocks. This has already happened in the Pacific Northwest, where hatchery-reared salmon are believed to have contributed to the region's salmon decline. The Pacific Northwest has more hatcheries than anywhere else, but very few salmon.

Biologists in Alaska are also worried about the hatchery-stocking program of salmon. One river in the Kenai Peninsula, the Ninilchik, has received hatchery stockings of king salmon since 1987, and catches have risen eight- to ten-fold, but the big hatchery return may be about to overwhelm the river's natural run of kings and the genetic diversity of the river salmon and steelhead runs may be weakened as it has been in Washington and Oregon. To correct the situation, Alaska is cutting back from 250,000 to 50,000 king salmon released annually on the Ninilchik River.

Similar problems are occurring in California. For example, the Irongate Dam on the Klamath River had 40,000 salmon arrive at the hatchery in 1995, although only about 8,000 fish could provide the ten million eggs necessary for spawning. Moreover, during the two preceding years, far more fish had returned than ever before, so many were locked out in the river, causing problems for the wild fish. The hatchery-bred fish were swimming downstream to the Shasta River and other tributaries and breeding or competing for spawning space with wild salmon.

The California Department of Fish and Game (DFG) now says it will re-evaluate its hatchery management policies. It will also consider ways to begin tagging or fin clipping all hatchery-bred fish to make them easily identifiable when they are caught. Laws may be needed to protect the genetic diversity of wild salmon and allow only hatchery-bred salmon to be caught.

If we go on just breeding hatchery-raised salmon and not protecting wild salmon, eventually there will be no wild salmon left, and then the weakened hatchery-bred salmon will disappear because they do not have the genetic diversity to sustain themselves in the wild.

Protection of the Environment

California's Department of Fish and Game (DFG) is entrusted with protecting the fish and game of the state of California. It is run by a political appointee of the governor, who, historically, has been more beholden to the governor and to California politics than to the welfare of the state's fish and game resources, including salmon. The DFG is funded largely through the sale of fishing and hunting licenses. Fishing licenses in 1999 cost $27.55, making it one of the most expensive fishing licenses in the United States. The key to the survival of salmon is the survival of its habitat. The pollution industrial wastes, pesticide runoff from agriculture. and petroleum products from rain runoff on urban streets are all serious threats .Many cities are just now educating their citizens about the harm to fish from dumping old oil and other toxic wastes down sewer drains.

Another source of pollution is the dumping of dredge spoilings into San Francisco Bay off Alcatraz. These dredge spoilings from the harbors are highly toxic because they contain many heavy metals that have sunk to the bottom of the bay. They cloud the water with a film of silt that poisons small bait fish, such as anchovies, sardines, shiner perch, and shrimp, that provide food for salmon and other fish. For years fishermen—sport, party boat, and commercial—have protested the dumping of dredge spoilings in San Francisco Bay and even in the ocean waters.

Water is one of the most important resources for salmon's survival. Dams have blocked much of the original spawning habitat and prevented the heavy winter and spring flows from cleansing the rivers. Much of the water from the Sacramento and San Joaquin Rivers' drainage is sent south for residential and irrigation purposes. The lower water flows concentrate pollutants, raise water temperatures, and allow silting of the spawning beds .

Large water-holding companies are planning to buy islands in the San Joaquin–Sacramento River Delta that are below the river level, build dikes around them, and flood them during the winter rainy season. The companies plan to hold this water in the reservoirs of their private flooded islands and in the summer to pump the water into the canals and send it south, thereby getting around the prohibition against pumping water out of the river during the summer when the flow is low. The companies justify this plan by saying that without the reservoirs, the excess water from the winter rains would just drain away into the ocean. However, these heavy winter flows are necessary to scour out the gravel spawning beds of the river, to scour out the pollutants in the river bottoms, and to help flush the small salmon smolts out to sea.

Another problem associated with the loss of water is the pumping stations that pump the water into the canals to send south. These pumping stations suck up millions of small salmon every year and grind them up in the pumps, making them into pulverized fish meal. There is much more that can be done to make sure that the pumps are turned off when the salmon are in the rivers or that screens are in place to prevent the small salmon from being sucked into the pumps.

The building of dikes has also damaged salmon's habitat. The Sacramento River has changed over the years from a river that periodically flooded its banks and was bordered by shrubs and marshes that provided a rich environment for the survival of salmon. Today, it is almost entirely bordered by dikes—piles of concrete that prevent it from flooding over its banks. The concrete protects property and people in the low-lying areas surrounding the river, but it is not a good habitat for salmon. The trees and shrubs that once provided the habitat for aquatic life and shade to cool the water—both necessities for the salmon's survival—have largely disappeared along the banks of the Sacramento River.

Another obstacle to the salmon's survival are the dams placed on the Russian River from May through September to create swimming beaches and lakes. These dams prevent small salmon from migrating downstream. There have been lawsuits initiated to stop them.

Photo 10-2: Some nice-sized salmon just landed off San Francisco.

Logging practices including extensive roads are also a detriment to the salmon's habitat. Many areas of the watershed have been logged so poorly that when the rains come, the topsoil is washed into the rivers, forming a silt that covers the gravel that is necessary for the salmon to spawn .

The National Marine Fisheries Service has developed a recovery plan to protect and restore spawning and rearing habitat of the endangered Sacramento River winter-run Chinook Salmon. This plan is a good model for benefitting all salmon.

1. Provide suitable water temperature for spawning and rearing conditions.

2. Provide optimum flows in the Sacramento River.

3. Preserve and restore riparian (streamside) habitat.

4. Protect and maintain gravel resources.

5. Preserve and restore tidal marsh habitat.

6. Reduce pollution from Iron Mountain Mine

7. Reduce pollution from industrial, municipal and agricultural sources.

8. Reduce habitat loss, entrainment, and pollution from dredging operations.

9. Provide suitable water quality in the Sacramento River- San Francisco Bay system.

Nature has taken millions of years to create a fish as beautiful and hardy as the salmon, able to survive all of nature's cycles. There are no shortcuts to sustaining nature. Using shortcuts to make up for destroying the harmony of nature does not work. We need to reconsider what we have done by destroying the habitat and the spawning beds, by destruction of streamside   vegetation, and by the diversion of massive amounts of water for agriculture and development. Until these policies are corrected, salmon are going to have a difficult time surviving.

Chapter Eleven: The Making of a Salmon Fisherman

How I Learned to Love Fishing, 119 • The Temptation of Commercial Fishing, 121 • In Defense of Fishing and Hunting, 122

This final chapter is about how I became a fisherman who is passionate enough about salmon fishing to want to write a book about it and share what I have learned. Every fisherman has his or her own story, and perhaps my story will spark memories of your own and thoughts about what fishing means to you.

How I Learned to Love Fishing

I am not exactly sure when I learned to love fishing. My first memories are walking over a bridge in New Orleans with my mom at maybe age 2 and looking at the Mississippi River. I don't recall any fish in those memories, but in my mother's womb I had gills while I was developing.

When I was about 4 years old, I moved to the Southern California town of Ontario and lived with my grandfather, who farmed roses. This was desert country —not exactly the land of fishing. But my grandfather, who grew up in Russia and immigrated to the United States around the turn of the century, would tell me stories about his childhood, when he used to hang out by the docks on the river and watch people fish and dream of fishing. He was too poor to afford fishing tackle, so he pulled hairs out of horses' tails. He had to sneak up on the horse without the owner noticing and sharply pull out a long hair. When he got three or four hairs, he tied them together to make a line. Then he would look for a pin to bend into a hook and catch a fly or some other insect to use as bait, and that was all he needed to catch little fish off the dock. My grandfather passed his love for fishing to me through these stories, and I asked him to tell them to me over and over.

The first fish I remember catching was in the irrigation water at my grandfather's farm. The water was stored in a reservoir and when he irrigated, it came through standpipes into the fields. When I was about 5 years old, I was playing in the water coming out of the standpipes, and I noticed some tiny minnows, perhaps half an inch long, swimming around. I put an old tin can in the water and when the minnows swam in, I lifted it out and caught two or three of them—the first fish I ever caught. I was so proud of them. I took them home, put them in a large glass jar and watched them, and finally I let them go back into the irrigation water.

A year or two later, I went with my grandfather to the reservoir near our house where the irrigation water was stored. In that reservoir were bullhead catfish and a few bass. We used worms we had dug up in our backyard and long cane poles with a hook, line, and bobber. We must have caught 10 or 15 bullhead catfish—about a half a pound each—in a couple hours. I was so excited to be catching fish on a line and feeling them tug at the pole! I was hooked on fishing.

I can still remember the first trout that I caught, around this same time. I went on a trip with my father to Bishop, California, in the Inyo Valley on the eastern side of the Sierras. I had a fishing pole and put a worm on a hook and threw it out into the current in the creek that ran by our motel. I watched the worm float slowly down with the current along the bottom in the crystal-clear water. Out from the bank darted a 6- or 7-inch brown trout; it grabbed the worm. I felt the tug as it darted back and forth, and I finally landed it. I sat there admiring its red spots and then showed it to my father. We cleaned it and had it frozen by the motel so that I could take it home. I was never so proud of a fish as I was of that beautiful little trout.

Growing up in Southern California, I had few opportunities for fishing. What there was, I made the best of. I caught trout in the creek flowing out of Mount Baldy, about 20 miles north of town. To the south about 10 miles was the Santa Ana River—not much of a river, probably 6 inches deep and 50 to 60 feet wide with a sand bottom, but it flowed all year long, and during winter storms, it even flooded the banks. Along both edges were channels 2 to 3 feet deep under the brush, where catfish and small rock bass abounded. Starting at age 11 or 12 and continuing through high school, my friends and I went down there to fish. We caught crawdads or used worms to catch bluegill, rock bass, and catfish, and once in a while a large carp.

During these years, my grandfather introduced me to saltwater fishing. Several times a year, he chartered a boat and took his workers on a saltwater fishing trip, usually out of San Clemente, Oceanside, or San Pedro, where we fished for calico bass, barracuda, white sea bass, and yellowtail. The Southern California kelp beds were full of fish in the 1950's. On these trips, we filled gunny sacks with fish, and I had the time of my life.

I also remember trips with my grandfather and father and mother to Ensenada, Mexico, where we fished for the same fish, which were even more abundant. In Mazatlán, Mexico, where my father's sister lived, I was introduced to the deep-blue offshore waters of the Pacific Ocean and caught my first sailfish; it was over 100 pounds—an exciting feat for an 11-year-old. I also saw manta rays, all sorts of new types of birds, and dorado, or dolphin fish, which were a beautiful golden-green color, an experience that greatly enhanced my appreciation of the sea and the life in and around it.

During high school I sometimes went fishing for yellowtail at the Coronado Islands out of San Diego. I caught three or four 20-pound yellowtail that I thought would pull me into the ocean. Occasionally, we went 20 to 40 miles offshore to find the warm blue water where 15- to 30-pound albacore tuna lived.

By the time I was 18 and moved away to college at U.C. Berkeley, I was stricken by fishing fever, but I was unable to do much fishing because I had to study and work on weekends to support myself. Even though I was living on San Francisco Bay, which abounded with striped bass and salmon, I was unable to afford the party boats that went fishing for them. Most of my fishing during these years was for trout in the Sierras or on the rivers in the Bay Area foothills.

I had never caught a salmon and my only knowledge of them was from reading the Southern California fishing reports. But I had always dreamed of catching one. One of the foremen who worked for my grandfather used to go salmon fishing every year on the Klamath River and come back with stories of 20-, 30-, and 40-pound salmon that he caught.

Finally, when I moved to San Francisco in 1962 to go to dental school, I was introduced to salmon fishing. I had discovered a place south of San Francisco along the coast, in Pacifica, at a beach called Linda Mar near Pedro Point, where a woman rented out six to ten wooden rowboats she kept on a wooden deck near her house. From her deck, she had built a launch ramp made of greased, skinned eucalyptus trees 6 to 10 inches in diameter, placed a couple feet apart. The rowboats were slowly slid down into the water, with a rope attached to the bow and a winch at the top of the ramp. Once the boat was down to the end of the ramp, it had to be quickly turned around so that the bow was facing into the waves. Then you had to row out through the breakers, timing it so that a wave didn't break on top of your boat.

Most of the people who rented boats here had outboard motors. After rowing past the breakers, they started their motors and headed for the fishing grounds, which were very close in, from several hundred yards to several miles. But I did not have an outboard motor, so I rowed.

My friends and I learned by watching the other fishermen. They did what was called "trolling," using 2- to 3-pound weights with a sinker release and anchovies on a heavy rod and reel. We did the best that we could with our lighter weights (1/2- to 1-pound), which we lowered 20 to 30 feet behind the boat, and then tried trolling by rowing. What we were actually doing was "mooching." We were probably the first moochers in the San Francisco Bay Area.

We were able to start trolling after I found an old, abandoned rowboat up by the Sacramento River and brought it home and repaired it. We bought a used outboard motor for about $15, and after figuring out how to get the heavy boat into the ocean and how to bail it out at a steady rate, we managed some successful trips.

At Linda Mar I had many experiences, including having my boat swamped in the breakers. I knew little about the sea or sailing, and I had to learn from the school of hard knocks and by what other people could tell me. We learned that if we caught a set of waves just right and rode a wave with the outboard motor going full speed, we could simply tilt the outboard up and surf the wave right into the sand. But I also learned that this method wasn't foolproof. One day when I went with my first wife, Lee, the surf was a little bigger than usual, but outside the large breakers the sea was calm and we spent all day on the water, caught several nice salmon, and headed back in. The swells were still quite large, but the engine was running just fine, so we picked out one at the end of a set. As we started surfing it in, what little gas was left in the gas can ran down to the front end and the motor didn't get any more gas. About two-thirds of the way in on the wave, the motor quit. The boat turned sideways as the wave passed under us, and we were sitting ducks for the next breaker. Being a good swimmer, Lee jumped out of the boat, just before the wave crashed on us. But I sat there, took the breaker like a man, and watched it destroy the boat and soak all the equipment. Because the boat was in only five or six feet of water, it quickly washed ashore. We recovered most of the equipment, including the drowned outboard motor (which never worked very well again) and most of our fishing equipment, and said good-bye to the destroyed rowboat that had served us faithfully, even though it had to be bailed out regularly.

After I graduated from dental school, I spent almost two years working in London. When I returned to San Francisco, one of the first things I did was head down to Linda Mar. The boats and the property had been sold, and there were no longer any rental boats available. People who owned boats kept them there for a monthly fee. There was no way to fish this area without my own boat.

So I bought my first boat—a 15-foot dory—with a well for the outboard motor. It was fairly heavy, built of plywood, and could be rowed through the surf and carried on a trailer. I launched it through the surf and through harbors on launch ramps. This dory gave me access to many fishing spots along the Northern California coast—from Half Moon Bay to Pedro Point, out of San Francisco and Sausalito, and up to Shelter Cove in Northern California. I fished salmon in all these places with my dory. I even got interested in commercial fishing and got a commercial license for the dory and started commercial fishing with hand lines for salmon.

The Temptation of Commercial Fishing

Most serious salmon fishermen who have owned their own boat have at one time or another considered commercial fishing. You are fishing salmon because you love it—but it is expensive, especially with your own boat, which costs a lot both to buy and to maintain. And then you have to buy gas, bait, fishing tackle. It all adds up to a lot of money.

Like a gold miner or a gambler, you always hear about those who have struck it rich. So and so had 2,000 pounds of salmon in one day. You multiply that by $2 per pound— that's $4,000 in one day! Then you think about all the expenses you can write off, and the attraction becomes even greater. There is also something very romantic about making a living fishing salmon. You are doing what you love: You're outdoors, on the sea, in tune with nature, your own boss, free at last. Before you know it, you're hooked.

Photo 11-1: A commercial salmon troller working the waters off San Francisco.

So in 1969 I bought a 28-foot commercial salmon troller. It was a converted Columbia River gill-netter made of Port Orford cedar over an oak frame. It was powered by a 6-cylinder Chrysler Crown gas engine with a 2:1 reduction gear and made about 8 knots at top speed. It had a cabin with a galley and water and a forward berth that could sleep one and a half small people.

It was fully equipped for salmon fishing with a compass, an automatic pilot, an old ship-to-shore radiotelephone, a depth finder, and three steering stations—one in the house, one on top on the flying bridge, and one aft in the fishing cockpit. It had not one, but four spool gurdies running off the stern, powered by a power takeoff connected to the propeller shaft by a chain. (Gurdies are small winches that carry 500 feet of cable to which you attach a large weight of up to 50 pounds and run hook and lines off it every 15 or 20 feet. So if you are fishing in 200 feet of water, you can run ten lines off each cable and cover all the depths from bottom to top.)

My boat, like most trollers, had outrigger poles that spread out the lines so that they covered more area and did not get tangled. It also had "flopper-stoppers," or stabilizers that hung off the outriggers and kept the boat from rolling side to side. There it was, fully equipped and just waiting to start hauling in those salmon. All I needed was a Brink's truck to carry the sacks of money to the bank.

Well, like a gold miner, I learned that equipment was just a small part of the job. No one told me about the hard work, long hours, getting up at 4 a.m., fishing all day, getting in at dark, and being too exhausted to even eat the undersized salmon I'd saved for dinner. No one told me about going to sleep in dirty, fishy-smelling clothes, only to be awakened by the noise of the other boats the next morning at 4 a.m. No one told me about doing this day after day. And no one told me that the daily reality wasn't 2,000 pounds of salmon, but that I would doing great if I got 100 pounds—and some days no one in the fleet caught any. Where was all the money? This was the easy life? The fact is that there are only a few days each season when the fishing is really hot—maybe ten or twelve days all year. But you have to be ready every day so you'll be there on those days.

Few fishermen are able to make a living fishing salmon. Most do it as a supplement to other jobs or other types of

TABLE D-7. **California** salmon **troll boat-size catch** statistics in pounds of dressed salmon.[a] (Page 1 of 2)

Year	Length Category (feet)	Number[c]	Percentage	Average Per Boat (pounds)	Total (pounds)	% of Total
		Vessels			Catch[b]	
1997[d]	≤20	51	6	1,164	59,372	1
	21-25	199	24	2,732	543,651	10
	26-30	122	15	4,530	552,603	11
	31-35	147	18	6,141	902,662	17
	36-40	156	19	8,633	1,346,716	26
	41-45	79	9	11,055	873,351	17
	46-50	56	7	13,191	738,704	14
	51-55	12	1	11,141	133,692	3
	>56	10	1	10,475	49,344	1
	Unknown	0	-	-	-	-
	TOTAL	832		6,250	5,200,094	

Diagram 11-1: The commercial catch by boat size in California, 1997. (Graph courtesy of the California Department of Fish and Game.)

fishing. Lots of them do it part time as a hobby or a tax write-off. I was one who didn't make a living, didn't strike it rich, and didn't get any tax write-offs, I just lost money, and the grueling work took the fun out of it.

I sold the 28-foot commercial troller and bought a small wooden dory that I could launch through the surf, put on a trailer, and tow anywhere salmon were biting. I got a commercial license, hooked up some hard lines with progressive weights that allowed me to troll multiple lines to depths up to 100 feet. I was a small, mobile commercial fisherman, one who could sport fish. If I caught a lot, I could sell them. I don't think I actually ever caught enough to sell, so I became in fact a sport fisherman, fishing for the enjoyment of it and enjoying it.

Today many small boats up and down the California coast commercial fish, or at least have commercial licenses. One of the most popular is the 16-foot Boston Whaler, and many other types, from dories to deep-V 16- to 25-footers, are used. The growing popularity of mooching has helped small boats. They wait until there is a hot bite and then take a few days off and fish. They may only fish ten or twelve days a year, but if they hit the bite right, they can bring in a few thousand extra dollars. And then they can deduct their expenses.

The larger commercial salmon trollers—those from 30 to 60 feet long—are responsible for about 80% of the commercial catch (see Diagram 11-1). About 300 commercial trollers fish the Bay Area. They are hard working, put in long hours, and have to love the sea to be able to do this job. They are the allies of those who want to save the salmon. If the salmon go, then their jobs and their way of life goes. They are a strong force through their union to protect the resource. They lobby to improve habitat, stop pollution, increase water flows, and, in general, look after the best interests of the salmon. It is up to the Department of Fish and Game and the National Marine Fisheries Service to manage the resource and set regulations to allow a certain percentage of the salmon to be caught, leaving enough making it up river to spawn and supply the hatcheries with all the salmon they need.

In Defense of Fishing and Hunting

Why? Is it humans? They were part of the scheme once, native to the land, brave and humble players. What is this curse we all suffer through them? Why must it be so? Do our people have to go down to dim perdition, never to show our brilliant silver sides to any eyes anywhere in the universe? Will not even the humans lament our passing?

—Queen Salmon, David Simpson and Jane Lapiner

Jacques Cousteau once stated that "fishing is hunting," fishing is more than killing a fish and eating it. For me, fishing is feeling one with nature. It is understanding and learning about the habits and life of one species of fish, in this case, the king salmon, and pursuing a relationship with it. In order to relate to the king salmon, you not only need to know as much as you can about the it, but you also have to know about nature—the ocean, the birds, the bait fish, the signs that indicate king salmon are around. King salmon are not just some creature swimming in the ocean. They are a part of nature, intimately related to the seasons and to the cycles of drought and flood. If we do not take care of the Earth, if we do not curb pollution, poor logging practices, and the damming of rivers without consideration for the fish that use them, then the salmon are doomed. In order to respect the quarry that we hunt or fish, we must also respect their habitat. We must respect nature and protect the Earth. We must become part of the cycle, part of nature.

We must become passionate in our defense of salmon. We must care, we must understand that what happens to salmon will happen to us. If salmon do not survive, then we will not survive. If we cannot protect the Earth enough to ensure that the salmon can spawn and reproduce, what will ensure that we humans will be able continue to spawn and reproduce? If we cannot protect our environment, if we allow it to be destroyed, so that the salmon, or other species do not exist, we are next. This is the source of the fisherman's spiritual communion with nature.

Who supports the salmon? Is it the uninterested masses? No, it is the fishermen, both commercial and sport, who give not only of their money through licenses but also of their spirit through caring. Sport fishermen buy licenses that supposedly help to provide for the management of the salmon. Commercial fishermen not only pay licenses but also have an assessment fee to help with stocking salmon through the hatcheries. Over 99% of the money used by the state of California to protect endangered species through oil-spill cleanup, toxic-spill inspection, streambed permits, and other non-game management and administrative costs comes from hunters and fishermen through their license fees. The average amount of money that the Department of Fish and Game gets each year from each hunter and fisherman is $35. The average resident taxpayer pays only eleven cents a year to help to manage the environment.

Anyone who is intimately related to fishing for a certain species, such as salmon, has a self-interest in protecting it. The extinction of the species would mean the end of their relationship with it. Therefore, they have a self-interest in keeping that species healthy and propagating in ever-increasing numbers. Salmon fishermen give back to nature by

Photo 11-2: The author with a 20-pound salmon caught mooching off the Marin County coast.

contributing to restoration of the habitat and to the setting up holding pens to raise salmon can be released into the ocean. Organizations that salmon fishermen belong to institute lawsuits that protect salmon by fighting poor logging practices, irresponsible dam building, pollution, and pumping stations that destroy juvenile salmon before they can get to the ocean.

What is the philosophy of salmon fishing? Unlike trout fishing, where catch-and-release fishing has caught on, salmon fishing is catch-kill-eat. There are biological reasons for this philosophy. Salmon live at most four or five years in the ocean and then go up river to spawn and die. There are more than enough salmon to go up river to spawn and perpetuate the species. The problem is all of the factors that prevent adult salmon from spawning and their eggs from hatching and prevent baby salmon from surviving to repeat the cycle.

The enjoyment that salmon fishermen get from pursuing, catching, and eating salmon is similar to that of a gardener who plants the seeds, watches the plants grow, picks the crop, and enjoys the bounty of the delicious meal that he or she has grown. We must give thanks to nature and to our hard work for the meal that we enjoy. It is part of the bounty of nature that has to be cherished and preserved, or else it will not exist forever.

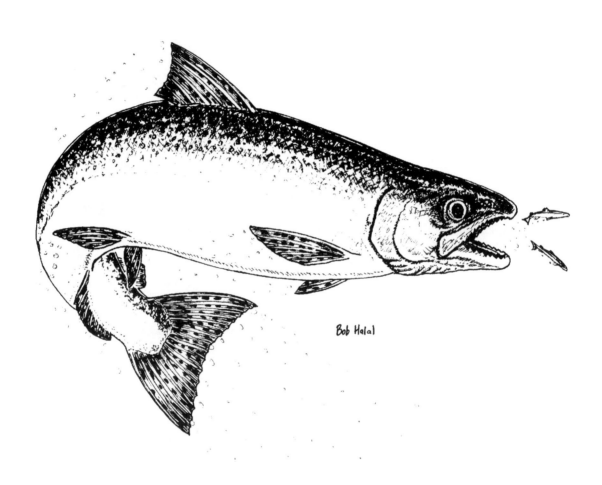

Bob Halal

Index of Charts and Maps

Bait Shops

Newport Beach to Point Conception: Southern California

Redondo Beach
Redondo Sportfishing (310) 372-2111, (310) 772-2064

Marina del Rey
Captain Frenchy's (310) 822-3625

Oxnard
Cisco's (800) 994-4852, (805) 985-8511

Santa Barbara
Sea Landing (Seahawk) (805) 963-3564

Point Conception to Pigeon Point: San Luis Obispo and Monterey-Santa Cruz

San Luis Obispo
Portside Marine and Tackle Shop (805) 595-7214

Morro Bay and San Simeon
Virg's Landing, Morro Bay (Mallard, Admiral) (805) 772-1222; (800) ROCKCOD

Monterey Bay-Santa Cruz
Santa Cruz Sportfishing (408) 426-4690
Bayside Marine (408) 475-2173
Breakwater Cove Deli (408) 375-6958
Fisherman's Supply (408) 476-5800
Andy's Bait and Tackle (408) 429-1925

Pigeon Point to Point Arena: Half Moon Bay, Gulf of the Farallones, San Francisco Bay and Delta, Bodega Bay

Half Moon Bay
Captain Pete, Quite a Lady (510) 339-6848
Captain John's (650) 726-2913
The Gear Store (650) 728-3055
Coastside #2 (415) 359-9790
Marine Warehouse (650) 728-7725

The Gulf of the Farallones: San Francisco, Emeryville and East Bay Ports, Sausalito
G and M Sales, San Francisco (415) 863-2855
Hi's Tackle Box, San Francisco (415) 221-3825
Jailhouse Bait and Tackle, Brisbane (415) 468-7887
Western Boat Shop, San Rafael (415) 456-5454
Loch Lomond Bait and Tackle, Loch Lomond (San Rafael) (415) 456-0321
Siegle's, Oakland (510) 655-8789

San Francisco Bay and Delta
G and M Sales, San Francisco (415) 863-2855
Hi's Tackle Box, San Francisco (415) 221-3825
Jailhouse Bait and Tackle, Brisbane (415) 468-7887
Western Boat Shop, San Rafael (415) 456-5454
Loch Lomond Bait and Tackle, Loch Lomond (San Rafael) (415) 456-0321
Siegle's, Oakland (510) 655-8789

Bodega Bay

The Boathouse (707) 875-3344
Porto Bodega (707) 875-3495
Wil's Fishing Adventures (707) 875-2323
Outdoor Pro Shop, Rohnert Park (707) 588-8033

Point Arena to Horse Mountain: Fort Bragg and Shelter Cove

Fort Bragg

Patty-C Charter Fishing, Noyo Harbor (707) 964-0669   Noyo Fishing Center, Fort Bragg (707) 964-7609
Fireo's Chevron Station (707) 964-5174

Eureka-Humboldt Bay

Bucksport Sporting Goods, Eureka (707) 442-1832
Eureka Fly Shop, Eureka (707) 444-2000
New Outdoor Store, Arcata (707) 822-0321
Pro Sport Center, McKinleyville (707) 839-9445
Roger's Market, McKinleyville (707) 839-3866

Trinidad

Salty's Sporting Goods, Trinidad (707) 677-3625
Bob's Boat Basin, Trinidad Harbor (707) 677-3625

Crescent City

Chart Room Marina, 130 Anchor Way, Crescent City 95531 (707) 464-5993
Crescent City Harbor, 101 Citizens' Dock Road, Crescent City 95531 (707) 464-6174
Sandie's Marine and Sport, Crescent City (707) 465-6499

Guide Services

Northern California Rivers: Smith, Klamath, Trinity, Eel, and Sacramento Rivers

Smith River

Gordy's Guide Service (707) 442-8904
Smith River Outfitters (707) 487-0935
John Woolworth Guide Service (707) 487-7571
Greg Nico Guide Service (707) 464-7320
Lunker Fish Trips (800) 248-4704
Bear Ridge Fishing Company (707) 539-9534
Steelie Dan's Guide Service (916) 684-7148

Klamath River

Gordy's Guide Service (707) 442-8904
Seiad Valley Guide Service (916) 496-3291
Steelie Dan's Guide Service (916) 684-7148
Bear Ridge Fishing Company (707) 539-9534
Northern California Guide Service (530) 527-9584

Trinity River

Gordy's Guide Service (707) 442-8904
Gerry Gray (888) 286-7250
John Rickey's Guide Service (530) 244-2494
Steelie Dan's Guide Service (916) 684-7148
God's Country Guide Service (916) 266-3297
Bear Ridge Fishing Company (707) 539-9534

Eel River

Gordy's Guide Service (707) 442-8904
Steelie Dan's Guide Service (916) 684-7148
Bear Ridge Fishing Company (707) 539-9534
Northern California Guide Service (530) 527-9584

Sacramento River

Steelie Dan's Guide Service (916) 684-7148
Northern California Guide Service (530) 527-9584
Iron Canyon Outfitters (888) 443-4748
Smith River Outfitters (707)487-0935
Bob's Guide Service (539) 222-8058
Sacramento Sport Fishing Guides (916) 487-3392
Rick Soto Fishing Guide (916) 226-0888
Free Willy's Guide Service (916) 529- 1233
M. L. Pound's Guide Service (916) 529-1233
Bear Ridge Fishing Company (707) 539-9534
Mike Bogue's Guide Service (916) 246-8457

Index